VOGT

LINKING LITERATURE AND WRITING

Integrating Literature Into Basic Skills Programs

by Shirley Cook with Kathy Carl

Incentive Publications, Inc.
Nashville, Tennessee

Illustrated by Marta Johnson
Cover by Tony Novak
Edited by Sally Sharpe

ISBN 0-86530-064-X

TABLE OF CONTENTS

FALL

September

October

November

WINTER

December

January

February

SPRING

March

April

May

PREFACE

LINKING LITERATURE AND WRITING contains integrated literature and writing activities designed for use in the primary classroom in conjunction with selected children's books. The major focus of the systematic model of instruction presented throughout this book is to promote the enjoyment of reading, to develop increased vocabularies, to enhance writing skills, to expand thinking skills, and to encourage a healthy self-concept. Because the activities offer practical applications of integrated curriculum in the areas of reading, writing and thinking, the teacher will find it easy to implement literature activities for all students!

Emphasizing literature in the primary grades is highly valuable. Literature enables students to enjoy stories with lasting value, to experience rich vocabulary, and to learn to share ideas with others. By responding to what they read, write, and think, students develop and hone critical and creative thinking skills. Literature also serves as a written model for young writers by concretely illustrating how to put thoughts on paper. Primary students need to experience the sense of authorship. As students write, they practice the skill of effectively communicating with an audience as well as gain an appreciation of the value of learning process skills. After continued reading of quality literature, individuals begin to experiment and practice new writing techniques. What's more, literature exposes students to beautiful illustrations which captivate students' interest, stimulate students' imaginations, and motivate students to explore their own capabilities.

Effective language arts instruction relies on the teacher's ability to "connect" literature and writing. LINKING LITERATURE AND WRITING contains the resources necessary to help students develop a holistic approach to reading and writing. These highly motivational activities will promote positive attitudes and increase the self-concept of every student!

HOW TO USE THIS BOOK

LINKING LITERATUE AND WRITING is divided into three sections — FALL, WINTER, and SPRING — for your convenience and easy use. Within these sections you will find literature and writing activities for every month of the school year.

TEACHER PAGES
Every teacher page is labeled with the month and theme. These pages contain the following components.

Synopsis
To quickly familiarize yourself with the selected book, read the brief story summary. Then formulate questions to ask the students in order to stimulate interest and excitement (see **Visuals** below).

Vocabulary
Review the vocabulary words with the class before reading the story. A worthwhile and beneficial activity is to have the students make vocabulary word books. Students write the story's vocabulary words in their books and "define" the words with picture cards, sentence games, synonyms, etc. Instruct the students to refer to their word books when they write.

Writing Activity
Each activity in this book integrates reading and the process of writing by using the following procedure:
1. The teacher reads a selected book.
2. The students discuss the book and complete a writing activity related to the story.

Curriculum Integration
As students become eager participants in the writing process, involve them further by implementing the suggested curriculum integration activity.

Visuals
The use of suggested visuals helps to motivate students and prepare them for the story and writing activity.

STUDENT PAGES
A number of the teacher pages are followed by reproducible student pages to be used in conjunction with the story. These pages are intended for reproduction and can be identified by this statement: © 1989 by Incentive Publications, Inc., Nashville, TN. All rights reserved.

HERBIE'S TROUBLES

by Carol Chapman

Synopsis
Herbie is having more than his share of problems. When everyone tries to give him advice about how his problems should be solved, Herbie finds that the best solution is to do what is most comfortable to him.

Vocabulary
1. assertive
2. definitely
3. granola bar
4. splattered
5. sprouted
6. tunnel

Writing Activity
Herbie's friends offer several solutions to his problems, but none of the solutions seems to work. Read the story up to the passage, "But he had to do what he had to do." Have the students fill out the "Herbie's Solution" student page. Discuss the students' ideas before continuing to read the story. Then read the remainder of the story to the class.

Herbie had to be able to solve his problems in a way that was comfortable to him. Ask the students to write their solutions for the problems on the *"Problems, Problems, Problems"* student page.

Curriculum Integration
Have the students draw pictures of "the schools of the future." Let the students discuss how the schools of the future would be different from the schools of today.

Visuals
- Let the students sample granola bars while you read the story.

Name _____

HERBIE'S SOLUTION

Herbie did not want to go to school if Jimmy John was to be there. If you were Herbie, what would you do?

_____

_____

_____

_____

_____

Draw a picture to show what you would do.

Name _____

PROBLEMS, PROBLEMS, PROBLEMS

1. If you just moved to a new school and didn't know anyone, how would you make new friends?

   _____

   _____

   _____

2. If someone at school, who claimed to be your good friend, was always copying your paper, how would you solve the problem without making your friend upset?

   _____

   _____

   _____

3. If someone in your class was constantly calling you a nickname that you didn't like, how would you get the person to stop without telling the teacher?

   _____

   _____

   _____

4. If your little brother or sister shared a room with you and always made a mess, how would you handle the situation?

   _____

   _____

MISS NELSON IS MISSING

by Harry Allard and James Marshall

Synopsis
The children in Miss Nelson's class learn nearly too late how fortunate they are to have such a fine teacher as Miss Nelson. Their eyes are opened by the fearsome Miss Viola Swamp.

Vocabulary
1. discouraged
2. misbehaving
3. refused
4. rude
5. tightly drawn
6. unpleasant
7. whizzed

Writing Activity
Stop reading the story when you reach page 24. Ask the students to describe another terrible trouble that may have befallen Miss Nelson. Miss Nelson's students suggest: a. "Maybe she was gobbled up by a shark"; b. "Maybe Miss Nelson went to Mars"; c. "Maybe Miss Nelson's car was carried off by a swarm of angry butterflies." Have the students illustrate their individual responses.

Curriculum Integration
Ask each student to create a thank-you card for someone he or she really appreciates but has not told so lately (see page 17). Have the students decorate their cards with bright colors and write one or two sentences inside the cards that say:
"Thank you so much for _____

_____ ."

Visuals
* Dress as Viola Swamp and read the story to the class.
* Draw attention to the book's illustrations.

THAT DREADFUL DAY

by James Stevenson

Synopsis

When the first day of school turns out to be just a little frightening, Grandpa is able to calm and reassure Louie and Mary Ann by telling a tale about his first day adventures of many years ago. His unusual tale causes Louie and Mary Ann to realize how lucky they truly are.

Vocabulary

1. absolutely
2. dense
3. dismal
4. dreadful
5. drizzle
6. dunce
7. generally
8. ghastly

Writing Activity

Stevenson has created a wonderful tale to share on the first day of school or any time during the first week. After reading the story, have the students complete the *"That Dreadful Day"* student page.

Curriculum Integration

Interviews can be a wonderful way to gather important information. Ask the students to interview their parents about what it was like when they were in school. Make a list of interview questions in advance. Questions may be brainstormed by individuals or the group. Discuss the interviews on the following day.

Visuals

- Relax and enjoy a fig bar break together!

Name _____

THAT DREADFUL DAY

1. On the first day of school, I really liked _____

    _____ .

2. My favorite time was when _____ .

3. One thing I didn't want to do was _____

    _____ .

Draw a picture to show something that happened on your first day of school.

THE OTHER EMILY

by Gibbs Davis

Synopsis
Emily loves being Emily, and she loves the T-shirt with her name on it. Emily's excitement on the first day of school changes to bewilderment when she encounters another Emily.

Vocabulary
1. aquarium
2. glowing
3. perfect
4. steamy
5. stomped

Writing Activity
Instruct the students to work on the *"Somebody Special's School Bag"* student page. Follow this with an oral discussion. Have each student write one sentence on the back of the student page concerning what he or she thinks is the most important item in his or her bag.

Then have the students complete the *"My Special Story"* student page.

Curriculum Integration
Ask the students to find out why they were given the names that they have. Instruct the students to try to find out what their names mean. Each student may then complete a speculative coat of arms regarding his or her family history.

Visuals
• Let the students "listen" to a large shell by placing their ears against the opening.

Name _____

SOMEBODY SPECIAL'S
SCHOOL BAG

Choose five important items to put in your school bag for the first week of
   school.
Color the items, cut them out, and glue them to the bag.
Tell why you chose each item.

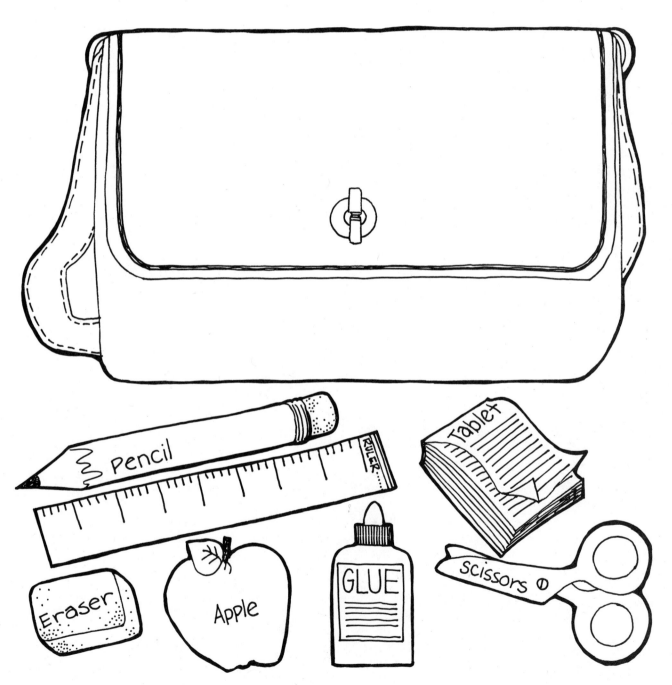

Name _____

MY SPECIAL STORY

On the way to school today, my friend and I saw _____ and

_____ . When we saw them, we wanted to _____

or _____ .

Then we saw our school. It looked _____ . We went inside

and found our class. The best thing that happened all day was

_____

_____ .

Draw a picture for your story here:

Name _____

COAT OF ARMS

1. In section 1, draw a picture of a mascot for your family.
2. In section 2, draw a suitable castle for your ancestors.
3. In section 3, draw a suit of armor that an ancestor could have worn for protection.
4. In section 4, draw your family.

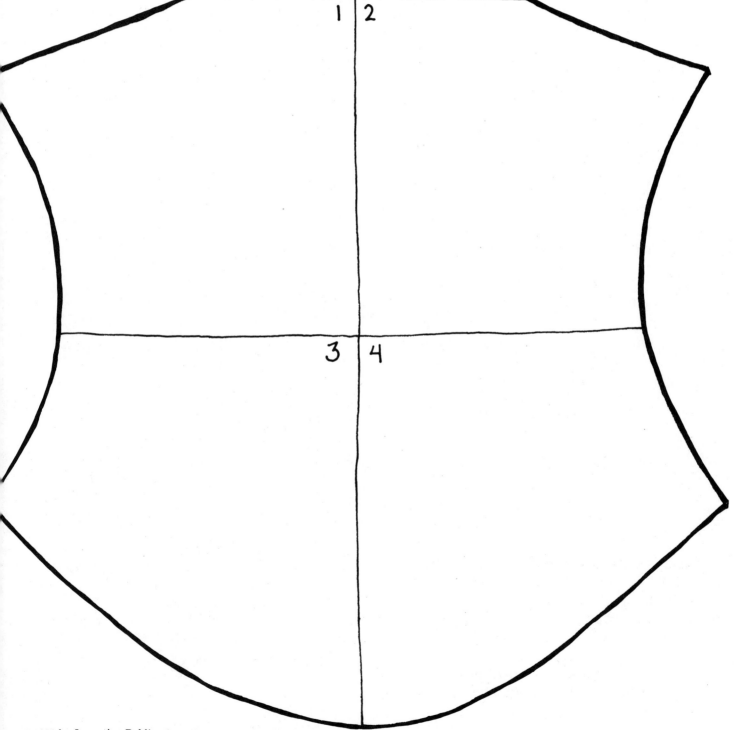

A CHAIR FOR MY MOTHER

by Vera B. Williams

Synopsis
When a fire destroys the home of a poor family of three generations of women, they must struggle to replace their few treasured possessions. By collecting the tip money from mama's job at the Blue Tile Diner, they are able to save enough money to buy a new stuffed chair.

Vocabulary

1.	armchair	6.	diner
2.	ashes	7.	exchanged
3.	bargain	8.	pumps
4.	charcoal	9.	tips
5.	delivered	10.	velvet

Writing Activity
Ask the students to close their eyes and to visualize a fire blazing through each of their homes one day while everyone is gone to school or work. Have them imagine that the fire destroyed everything they own. Ask each student to choose one item he or she would want to replace. Have the students complete the student page *"Replacing Something Special."*

Curriculum Integration
Have the students use watercolors to illustrate a scene from the book or a scene from the imaginary fires they visualized in their minds.

This is a good time to discuss fire safety. Students can create slogans that would be helpful in alerting others to fire hazards. The students can illustrate the slogans to create fire-prevention posters.

Visuals
- You may want to bring ashes or charcoal to class for a discussion.

Name _____

REPLACING SOMETHING
SPECIAL

If all of our belongings were destroyed in a fire, I would want to save

money to buy a _____

_____ .

I would want to buy it because _____

_____ .

It would look like this:

BEA AND MR. JONES

by Amy Schwartz

Synopsis
Bea and her father encounter new experiences when they switch places — Bea heads for the office while dad goes to school.

Vocabulary
1. advertising
2. astounding
3. blotter
4. business associate
5. campaign
6. challenge
7. deadline
8. dreadful
9. executive
10. extraordinary
11. introduced
12. lollipop
13. magnolia
14. matinee
15. memo
16. monitor
17. niche
18. promotion
19. thoughtfully

Writing Activity
Ask the students to complete the student page *"If I Could Switch."*

Curriculum Integration
Bea joined an advertising firm and wrote jingles to advertise products. Encourage the students to write jingles to advertise favorite products. Have the students illustrate the products. Brainstorm commercial advertisements before the students write their jingles.

Visuals
- Cut out pictures of timely advertisements to share with the class.

Name _____

IF I COULD SWITCH

1. For one day, I would like to change places with _____

   _____ .

2. I would like to do some of the things this person does such as

   _____

   _____ .

3. The hardest part about trading places with this person would be

   _____

   _____

   _____ .

4. The most exciting thing about trading places with this person

   would be _____

   _____

   _____ .

   This is a picture of me in my new "place":

BEST FRIENDS

by Steven Kellogg

Synopsis
Louise Jenkins is Kathy's best friend. They do absolutely everything together. When Louise goes to her aunt and uncle's home in the mountains for the summer, Kathy is trapped with strange new emotions in a lonely, deserted neighborhood.

Vocabulary
1. admit
2. allowed
3. contagious
4. jealous
5. lanyard
6. litter
7. lodge
8. pretend
9. rescue
10. reserve
11. resort
12. stallion
13. traitor
14. volcanic eruption

Writing Activity
Have the students discuss and illustrate this thought: Being a friend means _____ .

Ask the students to draw and write about an imaginary pet they would like to share with a friend.

Brainstorm with the students a list of characteristics that they would like new neighbors to have. Let the students illustrate their ideal neighbors and then tell about them.

Curriculum Integration
Discuss jealousy, anger, and happiness, noting how they are different. Discuss beneficial and non-beneficial emotions and how each emotion makes people feel. Have each student make a mask illustrating an emotion (see the next page). Reread the story, asking the students to put on their masks at the appropriate times.

Visuals
- Analyze the details in one of Kellogg's pictures.
- Display stuffed dogs or bring a real puppy to class.

THE BIG ORANGE SPLOT

by Daniel M. Pinkwater

Synopsis

In a neighborhood where all of the houses are exactly the same, Plumbean's creative home exterior provides an interesting topic of conversation for the neighbors. This is an excellent little story on conformity.

Vocabulary

1. belfry
2. hammock
3. nonconformist
4. sea gull
5. steam shovel

Writing Activity

Ask the students to think about how they would design the ideal house. What color would it be? What decorations would it have? What would be found in the yard? What size and shape would the house be? Instruct the students to write about and illustrate their ideal homes on the *"My Ideal House"* student page.

Curriculum Integration

Brainstorm ways a nonconformist might deal with a friend who wants him or her to ignore the new girl in school because she doesn't dress like the other children.

Visuals

- Cut out a large orange "splot" (orange felt) and duplicate three or four houses like those on Plumbean's street.

Name _____

MY IDEAL HOUSE

1. What shape would you choose for your house? _____

   _____

2. What color would you paint your house? _____

3. How would you decorate your house? _____

   _____

4. What would you have in your yard? _____

   _____

Draw a picture of your ideal house below.
Include as many details as you can.

I'M TELLING YOU NOW

by Judy Delton

Synopsis
Artie discovers that his mother hasn't told him everything that he should not do, and that he must make some common sense decisions on his own.

Vocabulary
1. breeze
2. China
3. decided
4. invited
5. leash
6. raspberry
7. shaded
8. whimper

Writing Activity
Ask the students to create illustrations of something that they know their mothers will not allow them to do (although the mothers may not have "said" it). Have each student write a few sentences describing what he or she is not allowed to do.

Curriculum Integration
If someone really were to "dig to China," what would he or she find in the dig? Give the students the time and the resources to "uncover" what they would find if it actually were possible to dig "straight through" the earth. Use a globe to predict where one would land if he or she were to dig straight through the earth beginning in front of your school.

Visuals
- a map of the world
- a globe

IF I WERE IN CHARGE OF THE WORLD

by Judith Viorst

Synopsis
This book is filled with delightful poetry about everything from a mother's not wanting a dog to the fantasies of a little girl who wants to change her name. Viorst's humor is right on target for both young and old.

Vocabulary
1. aching	5. fright	9. produce
2. cancel	6. giant	10. swollen
3. demon	7. heal	11. troll
4. disgraceful	8. mending	12. warlock

Writing Activity
Have the students complete the patterning project *"If I Were In Charge Of The World"* (below).

Curriculum Integration
Let each student share a book that is "Oh-Wow!" with a friend or a small group.

Visuals
- Before reading the poetry, have the children draw and color pictures of things they would change if they were in charge of the world. Have the students share their pictures.

Patterning Project

If I Were In Charge Of The World

I'd cancel	There'd be	You wouldn't have

IRA SLEEPS OVER

by Bernard Waber

Synopsis
Ira decides to spend the night with his friend Reggie. Because it is Ira's first night at a friend's house, he must confront the problem of what to do with his beloved teddy bear, his nightly "security blanket."

Vocabulary
1. collection
2. dominoes
3. magnifying glass

Writing Activity
Have the students put themselves in Ira's position and write letters to Dear Abby about the teddy bear problem. Then ask each student to assume the identity of Dear Abby and answer someone else's letter.

Curriculum Integration
Help the class investigate the origin of the teddy bear.

Make dough teddy bears using the following recipe:

1 cup flour
1/2 cup salt
3/4 cup water

Mix the ingredients. Add more water or flour as needed. Shape the dough into the form of a bear. When finished, bake at 300 degrees for about two hours. Add food coloring to the dough before baking or paint the dough after baking.

Visuals
- a favorite stuffed bear
- a security blanket
- a picture of a child with a security blanket

I'M TERRIFIC

by Marjorie Sharmat

Synopsis

Jason Everett Bear thinks he is so terrific that he awards himself gold stars for the wonderful bear that he is. His neighbors don't agree that he is terrific. Jason experiences some interesting changes as he attempts to find out who he really is.

Vocabulary

1. admire
2. appreciate
3. bureau
4. clobber
5. disposition
6. fantastic
7. gathering
8. incredible
9. industrious
10. instant
11. introduce
12. occasionally
13. ridiculous
14. spare
15. tidy

Writing Activity

Shape books are always great fun for kids. Use the bear pattern on the following page to make shape books. Encourage the students to write adventures about a bear. (Bears must, of course, be given appropriate names.) Cut writing paper to fit the shape of the bear pattern and use the pattern to make covers for the mini-books.

Curriculum Integration

Have each child make a list of things that he or she does well and a list of things that he or she would like to do better. Ask each student to illustrate one of the things on each list.

Visuals

- stuffed bears
- gold stars for each student
- Chorao's illustrations

THE LUCKIEST ONE OF ALL

by Bill Peet

Synopsis
Just who is the luckiest one of all? View the state of the world through the eyes of a boy, a bird, a bass, and a long series of creatures wishing to be someone or something else.

Vocabulary

1. beacon	8. glimpse	15. miserably	21. swarm
2. bedraggled	9. impudent	16. pell-mell	22. sycamore
3. boast	10. incredibly	17. rambunctious	23. task
4. commotion	11. inquisitive	18. sprite	24. thrush
5. cumbersome	12. lumbering	19. stately	25. toting
6. frenzy	13. lure	20. stroll	
7. frothing	14. midst		

Writing Activity
The story is written as a circle story. It begins and ends at the same point after taking a journey to many additional places. Students may enjoy writing an additional part for the circle concerning another person or thing. For example, the jet plane might wish to be a spaceship which might in turn wish to be a cloud. The students may write their additions in rhyme or in prose.

Curriculum Integration
Students can put together collages of magazine pictures that represent things that the students would like to be.

Visuals
- other books by Bill Peet

MAUDE AND SALLY

by Nicki Weiss

Synopsis
Best friends Maude and Sally do everything together. However, when Sally goes away to summer camp, Maude plays with Emmylou. Upon Sally's return, a wonderful change takes place.

Vocabulary
1. aisle
2. collection
3. concerned
4. foreign accent
5. perfect match
6. phoney
7. saddle shoes
8. satin
9. separate
10. triplets

Writing Activity
Students will enjoy writing thank-you notes to special friends to tell them how much they are appreciated. (Use the *"I-Care-O-Gram"* forms on the following page.)

Curriculum Integration
Students will enjoy experimenting with the art of costume design. Ask the students to illustrate simple two or three-part costumes for children.

Organize a "friends" lunch to be held the day after you read the story. Each child should bring his or her favorite kind of sandwich. Let pairs of students sit together during lunch and exchange sandwich halves. (Inform parents in advance of this activity.)

Visuals
- satin
- saddle shoes
- the book's illustrations

I-CARE-
O-GRAM

To:
From:

I-CARE-
O-GRAM

To:
From:

MY FRIEND JACOB

by Lucille Clifton

Synopsis
Jacob and Sam are not only next door neighbors, but are very best friends as well. They are friends who are always helping each other. One day, Sam decides to help Jacob learn to do something that Jacob has never done before. The surprise ending will warm your heart.

Vocabulary
1. celebrate
2. decided
3. especially
4. notices
5. probably

Writing Activity
Demonstrate how to fold a piece of drawing paper into fourths. Then have each student fold a piece of paper into fourths and draw in each section a picture of something that friends can do together. Instruct the students to write one or two sentences about each activity under the picture.

Curriculum Integration
Discuss handicaps. Have the class brainstorm a list of ways that handicapped and non-handicapped persons are the same.

Learn to sing a song or message for a friend or a group of friends.

Visuals
- Bring to class an object that was made by a handicapped person.
- Show illustrations of persons with handicaps.

MOTHER TOLD ME SO

by Carrol A. Marron

Synopsis
Although Mother has told her daughter that she (Mother) was nearly perfect as a child, Grandma "spills the beans" in this delightful tale of youthful pranks.

Vocabulary
1. dropping
2. graceful
3. hamper
4. perfect
5. rubber plant
6. scamp
7. slopped
8. spider plant
9. stashed
10. turnstile

Writing Activity
Students will delight in writing a few sentences about things they have done that a "perfect" child would not do. Make a classroom booklet titled *"The Not-So-Perfect Child."* The students may illustrate their own contributions.

Amusing and amazing tales will result when students fill in this blank: I know that my mom/dad is not always perfect because Grandma (or other person) told me about when she/he _____ . Students may illustrate their sentences. (Be sure to share a not-so-perfect childhood experience of your own!)

Help the students create a list of rules that a "perfect" child must always follow. You may want to write this list on the board and have each student choose one rule to illustrate.

Curriculum Integration
The customs of a country sometimes may determine what rules are followed by the parents and children of that country. Search for a custom that is accepted as good behavior in another country, but that would be considered inappropriate behavior in the United States.

Visuals
- Show the students pictures of spiders and rubber plants. (If possible, show the real things!)

THE PATCHWORK QUILT

by Valerie Flourney

Synopsis

Tanya's grandmother has a dream — to create a patchwork quilt filled with family memories for her granddaughter. When Grandmother becomes ill, it looks as if the dream may not become a reality. Tanya is not about to let the treasured masterpiece remain unfinished. With the help of Mama and the rest of the family, Tanya is able to help Grandma realize her dream.

Vocabulary

1. absent-mindedly
2. blended
3. clutching
4. corduroy
5. department store
6. flexed
7. glint
8. hunched
9. masterpiece
10. mischievous
11. numb
12. pay respects
13. permitted
14. restlessly
15. tilted

Writing Activity

Cut 3" x 3" squares out of three colors of typing paper. (Each student will need 9 squares.) Instruct each student to write on each square a sentence or two telling about something memorable in his or her life or the life of a family member. Have the students detail each section with a mini-picture or a watercolor wash picture. Assemble the squares to make a quilt.

Curriculum Integration

Have each student prepare one quilt square depicting something that is important in his or her life. Assemble the squares into one large classroom quilt.

Example:

Visuals

- Bring a patchwork quilt or other homemade quilt to class.
- Prepare a sandwichboard paper quilt that you can wear as a display.

THE RELATIVES CAME

by Cynthia Rylant

Synopsis
When relatives from Virginia come to visit, hugs, laughter and music fill the house. All students will enjoy this heartwarming story about family visits.

Vocabulary
1. particular
2. relatives
3. Virginia

Writing Activity
Duplicate a set of paper dolls for each student using the patterns provided. (Each doll will represent a family member.) Students should decorate the fronts of the dolls with the appropriate personal details such as hair, eyes, clothing, etc. Have the students write the names of the relatives on the dolls. Students should write key words, phrases or sentences on the back of each doll to detail something memorable about that person.

Curriculum Integration
Challenge the students to point to states (on a map) in which their relatives live. Each student may want to research one of the key tourist attractions of a state he or she has named.

Visuals
- Share pictures of your relatives with the class.
- Use a large map to trace a route from Virginia to the approximate area where your school is located.

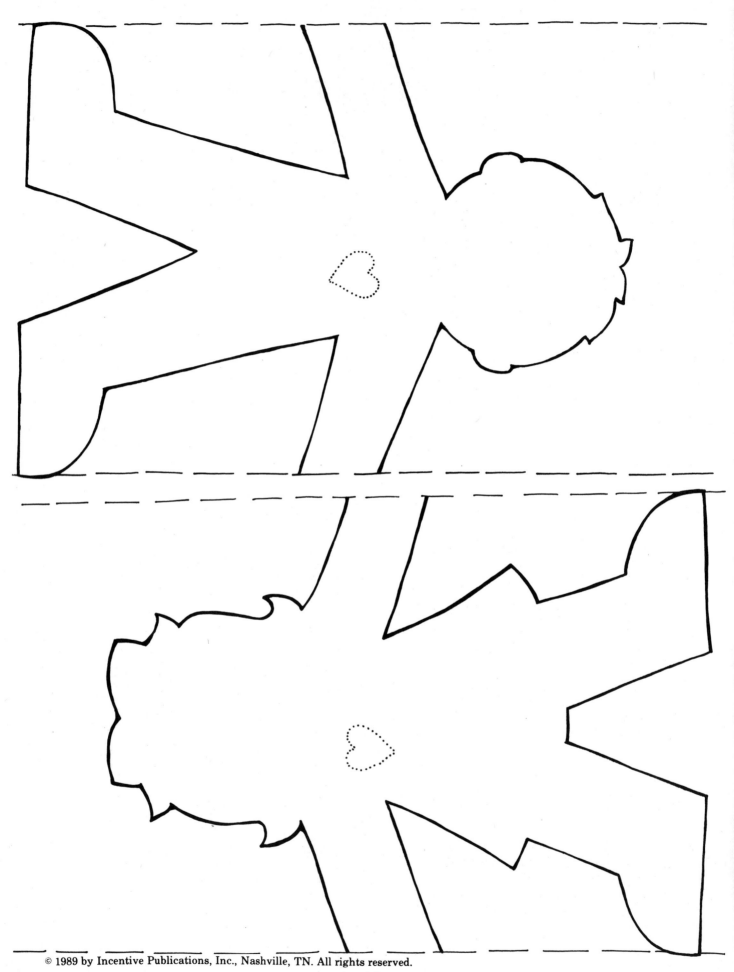

ROLLING HARVEY DOWN THE HILL

by Jack Prelutsky

Synopsis
In this comical story told in verse, Harvey is a scoundrel, a bully, and the nightmare of every child. Revenge is sweet the day they roll Harvey down the hill.

Vocabulary

1. apartment
2. bragging
3. buddies
4. cellar
5. competes
6. lard
7. latch
8. outfield
9. pest
10. positive
11. pranks
12. spoil
13. trousers
14. vacant
15. wander

Writing Activity
Ask each student to visualize four friends. Encourage the students to write two positive things about each friend and to illustrate those ideas.

I like John because _____

_____ .

Curriculum Integration
Show the students how to tie slip knots and square knots. (Demonstrate how to tie other types of knots, too.)

Visuals
• the book's illustrations

ROSIE AND MICHAEL

by Judith Viorst

Synopsis

Rosie and Michael have a special, close friendship. Their friendship is filled with humor, laughter, and sharing through good and not-so-good times.

Vocabulary

1. Costa Rica
2. dagger
3. dopey
4. droop
5. gushing
6. innocent
7. piranhas
8. pythons
9. shins
10. tidal wave
11. werewolves

Writing Activity

Each student should assume the identity of either Michael or Rosie. All "Michaels" should create a card to send to Rosie because she has broken her wrist. All "Rosies" should create a card to send to Michael because he has cut his head. Discuss greeting card jingles and share example cards with the class. Ask the students to include original humorous or serious jingles in their cards.

Curriculum Integration

Reproduce the friendship card on the following page for each student. Ask the students to follow these directions.

1. Fold the card.
2. Complete the statement on the front of the card.
3. Write a message to a special friend inside the card and add an illustration or design.
4. Write a joke or riddle on the back of the card.

Have the students create friendship pins by stringing small beads on mini gold safety pins. The students may attach the friendship pins to their cards (see spot indicated) and deliver them in person!

Give each student a copy of the *"Friendship Work Sheet"* to complete.

Visuals

- Display pictures of children working, playing, and communicating together.

Attach your friendship pin here.

Here's a joke or riddle for you:

Friends are important because:

YOU ARE MY FRIEND

From:_____

FRIENDSHIP WORK SHEET

Make a friendship word find puzzle.

Words to find:

1.
2.
3.
4.
5.
6.

Draw a picture on another piece of paper of something you and your
friend like to do together.

THE 329TH FRIEND

by Marjorie Sharmat

Synopsis

Emery Raccoon has a party for his 329 closest friends because he is looking for a special friend to keep him from becoming lonely. He soon discovers that he is a pretty fine friend for himself.

Vocabulary

1. definitely
2. guest
3. invite
4. possum

Writing Activity

Have the students complete the *"It's My Party"* student page.

Curriculum Integration

Instruct the students to research three "A,B,C Facts" about one of the animals mentioned in the book. For example, if a student chooses a bear, he or she should form three factual statements that begin with "B."

Visuals

- Show pictures of various animals found in the book (such as a possum).
- Share tarts or veggies with the class.

Name _____

IT'S MY PARTY

1. Pretend that you have decided to have a large party for your friends. Your guest list has 50 names on it. Name 10 of the people on your list.

   1. _____   6. _____

   2. _____   7. _____

   3. _____   8. _____

   4. _____   9. _____

   5. _____   10. _____

2. What four foods will you serve?

   _____   _____

   _____   _____

3. What preparations will you need to make for the party?

   _____

   _____

4. How will you entertain your guests?

   _____

   _____

   _____

5. Draw a picture of your party on the back of this paper.

I WAS A SECOND GRADE WEREWOLF

by Daniel Pinkwater

Synopsis

As strange as it may seem, Lawrence, an average second grade boy, turns into a werewolf during the night. When he awakens he is thrilled and can't wait for his family and friends to notice. What happens to Lawrence during his average "second grade day" is both interesting and amusing.

Vocabulary

1. werewolf	4. pretending
2. snarling	5. cellophane
3. strict	6. normal

Writing Activity

Children can analyze the advantages and disadvantages of becoming something else during the night and waking up with new characteristics. Ask the students to describe what they would most like to become if they could magically change for one day. Then they should illustrate "the new me" and write about three things that they would be able to do that they couldn't previously do.

Curriculum Integration

One class member may volunteer to be the "quick change artist." Allow the students to study that person carefully. Then ask the child to leave the room and change one thing about his or her appearance. (Shoes could be untied, a sock pulled up, etc.) When the child returns, have the students try to guess what change has been made.

Visuals

- Display pictures of werewolves.
- Show pictures that are nearly identical and ask the students to find the differences.

THE BABY UGGS ARE HATCHING

by Jack Prelutsky

Synopsis

Unusual cartoon characters move into action as Jack Prelutsky plays with a variety of rhyming words to create delightful poems. The descriptive language will paint a picture in the young reader's mind.

Vocabulary

1. absolute
2. creep
3. deplorable
4. despicable
5. disintegrate
6. excavate
7. glimpse
8. groan
9. guzzle
10. hatch
11. pulverize
12. scramble
13. searching
14. snatch

Writing Activity

Jack Prelutsky's story is filled with action words. Work as a class to generate a list of action words found in the story. Let each student draw a cartoon creature and write an action poem about the creature's movements.

Curriculum Integration

Create an illustrator's corner. Fill a table with multiple copies of cartoon drawing books (from the library). Place large strips of construction paper and "window boxes" cut out of white construction paper on a table for students to use in creating their own cartoon strips.

Visuals

- filmstrips on cartooning

THE DREAM EATER

by Christian Garrison

Synopsis

Yukio rescues a Baku who, in turn, devours the bad dreams of the villagers. Then the villagers may slumber peacefully, and the Baku is content.

Vocabulary

1. bandits
2. brimstone
3. contented
4. demon
5. devour
6. disturb
7. dragon
8. fierce
9. harvest
10. honored
11. longed
12. mending
13. morsel
14. Mount Fuji
15. munched
16. plentiful
17. preparing
18. samurai
19. tender
20. uneasy
21. weapon

Writing Activity

Have the students create character developments of another type of person or animal who could "get rid of" bad dreams. Students should draw pictures of the "Dream Eater" and list five of its most interesting characteristics.

Curriculum Integration

Find Japan on a map. Let the students investigate to find as much information as possible about Mt. Fuji. What are some Japanese customs that relate to Mt. Fuji?

Visuals

- other books about bad dreams
- pictures of Japanese villages

THE GREAT GREEN TURKEY CREEK MONSTER

by James Flora

Synopsis
A mysterious seed sprouts into a "Great Green Hooligan Vine" and spreads throughout the town. This hilarious story keeps young readers involved as they search for a solution to the problem.

Vocabulary
1. axes
2. blinked
3. earned
4. governor
5. knot
6. parade
7. principal
8. secret
9. slithered
10. trombone
11. vine
12. yank

Writing Activity
Discuss the problem of the story with the class. What was the cause of this problem? How did the green monster affect the town? What was the unusual solution to the problem?

Brainstorm things related to the color green.

Let the class create a green booklet. The students can write stories and poems about the color green or design pictures of things related to the color green.

Curriculum Integration
Use butcher paper to create a large green monster. Let each student cut large green scales out of tissue paper to be glued to the monster figure. The class will enjoy this bigger-than-life creation.

Visuals
• Decorate the room in green!

HARRY AND THE TERRIBLE WHATZIT

by Dick Gackenbach

Synopsis
Harry searches for his mother, but he is afraid to go down into the cellar. The two-headed Whatzit becomes very real to Harry as he explores the dark spaces.

Vocabulary
1. answered
2. believes
3. cellar
4. clawed
5. disappeared
6. discovered
7. furnace
8. pickles
9. terrible
10. worried

Writing Activity
Ask the students to share their experiences of being afraid. Discuss the feeling one has when he or she overcomes a fear.

Discuss this question:
Can people change their ideas about places, people, and feelings?
Ask the students to complete these sentences:

When I was younger, I liked to ____
_____ .
When I was younger, I was afraid to
_____ .
When I was younger, I felt _____ .

Curriculum Integration
Brainstorm ideas related to the word *change*. Ask the students to bring baby pictures of themselves to class. Everyone will enjoy seeing how classmates have changed.

Visuals
- Display pictures of and information about chameleons.
- Mount pictures of trees of every season on a bulletin board.

THE ISLAND OF THE SKOG

by Steven Kellogg

Synopsis

Jenny and her mouse friends decide that city life is far too dangerous, so they set sail on the high seas in search of a peaceful place to live. The island on which they land has only one problem . . . the Skog. The resolution of the problem is a joyful surprise.

Vocabulary

1. brilliant
2. cautiously
3. convinced
4. dedicated
5. faded
6. harbor
7. lurched
8. marooned
9. narrow escape
10. national anthem
11. pier
12. plunged
13. rodent
14. sand dune
15. tenderfeet
16. unprepared
17. waded

Writing Activity

Before reading the last page of the story, ask the students to create a national anthem for the island of the Skog. Additional projects might include the creation of a national flag or national flower (based on real or imaginary flowers and flags). Let the students share their creations orally.

Students may illustrate their own Skogs and describe the Skogs in brief paragraphs.

Curriculum Integration

Guide the students in researching islands of their choice to discover answers to the following questions:

1. Where is the island located?
2. Who discovered the island and when?
3. How would life have been different during the time of the island's discovery?
4. Who lives on the island now?
5. Approximately how far is the island from your school?

Visuals

- Kellogg's illustrations

JOEY RUNS AWAY

by Jack Kent

Synopsis
Joey, a young kangaroo, runs away from home after he is asked to clean his room. Many animals try to live in Joey's mother's pouch without great success during the ensuing comic misadventures.

Vocabulary

1. awful	7. heavy	11. nowhere
2. comfortable	8. jumble	12. pelican
3. crayon	9. moment	13. rent
4. decided	10. mumbled	14. scary
5. empty		

Writing Activity
Discuss the reason Joey ran away from home. Ask the students to share their feelings about running away from a problem. Work as a group to list Joey's solutions to his problem. Work through the following criteria chart to visualize the value of the solutions.

SOLUTION FINDING			
	Reasons or Criteria		
Ideas 1. 2. 3. 4. 5. 6.			Rank 1-6

Curriculum Integration
Place a large piece of poster board on the floor. Let the class work as a group to illustrate the mother kangaroo and all of the animals who attempted to live in her pouch. Encourage originality by allowing the students to illustrate additional animals that are not included in the story.

Visuals
• additional books by Kent

NO SUCH THINGS

by Bill Peet

Synopsis
Young readers will not stop laughing as Bill Peet's creatures come to life in a marvelous manner. The rhythmic verses are entertaining to read aloud or to act out as a group.

Vocabulary

1. amazing	6. ferocious	11. prairie
2. creatures	7. figure	12. reason
3. despair	8. guess	13. terror
4. enormous	9. haystacks	14. yawn
5. entire	10. perfect	

Writing Activity
The rhythmic verses found in *No Such Things* will stimulate the students' imaginations. Have the students list additional rhyming words on large tablets. Ask the students to exchange lists and to add phrases to the rhyming words. Share the results with the group.

Curriculum Integration
Have the students help to design an unusual imaginary animal. Cut four or more copies of this animal out of multi-colored paper. Let the students paint a landscape for the animals to explore. Glue the animals on the painting.

Visuals
- pictures of real animals
- filmstrips and books about landscapes

THE QUEEN OF EENE

by Jack Prelutsky

Synopsis

This book contains humorous poetry that will tickle the funny bone of any young person. Children will giggle aloud when Aunt Samantha wakes with a rhinoceros in her bed and Pumberly Pott's unpredictable niece takes things apart.

Vocabulary

1. axles
2. bureaus
3. chariot
4. creature
5. cushions
6. discreetly
7. dissolved
8. dreadful
9. fence
10. foolish
11. onion
12. polite
13. swallowed
14. unpredictable

Writing Activity

Discuss the "use" of humor in everyone's life. Ask each student to name the most humorous person in his or her family. Have the student explain why. Help the class create a humor survey. Allow the students to talk to classmates and to take the survey home. Survey questions might include:

Who is the most humorous person in your family?
Why do you feel humor is important to people?
The best joke I've heard lately is

_____ .

Each young writer should talk with at least five people and record their responses.

Curriculum Integration

Read pages 26 and 27 of *"The Pancake Collector"* and then use the following recipe to make a pancake snack:

Grandma's Pancakes

2 beaten eggs
1/3 cup sugar
1/2 tsp. salt
3 tbsp. butter
1 1/2 cups milk
2 cups flour
6 tsp. baking powder

Heat griddle to 350° F; grease lightly. Mix ingredients. Pour 1/4 cup batter for each pancake onto griddle. Turn pancakes when edges look cooked.

Visuals
- Show cartoon films.

THE WHINGDINGDILLY

by Bill Peet

Synopsis

A dog named Scamp wishes he could be a famous horse. Zildy the witch gets her magic directions a little mixed-up and Scamp becomes an extraordinary combination of many animals called a Whingdingdilly.

Vocabulary

1. admired	6. famous	11. miserable
2. dizzy	7. glance	12. pasture
3. dreary	8. gloomy	13. rambling
4. droopy	9. imitate	14. reflection
5. eager	10. magnificent	15. unsteady

Writing Activity

Give each student three large, colorful stars labeled ME, FAMILY, and THE WORLD. Ask the students to write a list of wishes on each star. Allow the students to share their lists.

Discuss the word *Whingdingdilly*. Ask the students if they believe Bill Peet created this word. Have students volunteer to create new words and to explain the words' "origins."

Curriculum Integration

Encourage students to create construction paper creatures having the body parts of many animals. Display the illustrations in a class Whingdingdilly art collection.

Remind the students of the rules of brainstorming: 1. Defer judgments. 2. List all ideas. 3. Encourage freewheeling. 4. Piggyback on others' ideas. 5. Strive for a large quantity of ideas. Have the students complete the following brainstorming activity.

Brainstorming Activity: List all things related to the word *wish*.

(Examples: wishbone, stars, when you wish upon a star, etc.)

Visuals
- constellation resource books
- animated animal pictures

AMANDA AND THE WITCH SWITCH

by John Himmelman

Synopsis
Amanda, feeling quite the generous witch, comes upon a toad and offers to grant him three wishes. The result is near catastrophe. However, Amanda proves to be a resourceful witch when she saves the day.

Vocabulary
1. antlers
2. decided
3. helpless
4. normal
5. pond
6. prank

Writing Activity
Reproduce the *"My Three Wishes"* student page for each student. Instruct the students to write three wishes that they would ask for if they were in the toad's place. The wishes should be for *changes* they would like to make, not for gifts or money. Students should write their wishes in complete sentences.

Curriculum Integration
Discuss how a graph is constructed and how it is of benefit in presenting information quickly and accurately. Have the students graph the differences between frogs and toads.

Visuals
- Use a magic wand to introduce the story.
- Show the pictures in the book.

Name _____

MY THREE WISHES

Write a wish in each star for a change you would like to make (not for gifts or money).

ARTHUR'S HALLOWEEN

by Marc Brown

Synopsis
Arthur is instructed to take his younger sister D. W. with him as he goes trick-or-treating. D. W. wanders into a house that the children believe is occupied by a witch. Arthur is forced to summon the courage to find her.

Vocabulary
1. aluminum foil
2. attendance
3. recognize
4. spooky

Writing Activity
Ask the students to take on the guise of newspaper reporters for a local newspaper. As reporters, the students are to cover the story of Arthur's Halloween adventure. Ask the students to pretend that they have interviewed Arthur himself.

As teacher, you may choose to take on the personality of Arthur and allow the group to conduct an interview before writing their stories.

Have the students write story headlines. (A folder of headlines clipped from newspapers will help the students "get the feel" of headline writing.) Each story should cover the five W's: who, what, when, where, and why.

Curriculum Integration
The silhouettes on the final page of the story clearly depict the characters. Let the students make silhouettes and mount the silhouettes on construction paper to send home as Halloween treats.

Visuals
• Let the students sample bat-wing brownies and vampire blood!

(Any brownie recipe will be fine. The brownies may be cut into the shape of a bat with a cookie cutter. Kool-aid makes good vampire blood.)

CRANBERRY HALLOWEEN

by Wende and Harry Devlin

Synopsis

When Cranberryport needs money to build a new dock, Mr. Whiskers volunteers to help raise the money. A mysterious attempted robbery is solved with surprising results.

Vocabulary

1. bogs	6. deserted	11. impatient	16. pursuing
2. burly	7. dismay	12. intentions	17. rascals
3. cellar	8. dock	13. in tow	18. scoundrel
4. chowder	9. donation	14. loomed	19. turrets
5. clam digger	10. gawked	15. passageway	

Writing Activity

Have the students draw pictures of the main characters in the story. Instruct each student to write one sentence describing each character in the picture.

Ask each student to create a set of construction paper lollipops. (Glue craft sticks to construction paper circles.) On each lollipop, the students must tell how a character "licked" a problem or "was licked" by a problem.

Curriculum Integration

Let the class work together to prepare one of the recipes on the back cover of the book.

Visuals

- Have cider and cranberries.

DORRIE AND THE GOBLIN

by Patricia Coombs

Synopsis
When a mischievous goblin suddenly appears and the sorcerer is not there to curb the goblin's evil ways, too much magic for any household occurs. Dorrie tries to tame her small charge while trying desperately to learn her new card trick before the big gala.

Vocabulary
1. banister	4. cauldron	7. gleamed	10. parlor
2. boiling	5. crystals	8. goblin	11. sorcerer
3. cancel	6. drapes	9. loomed	12. "ward it off"

Writing Activity
Divide the students into groups of three. Each group will need a piece of 12" x 18" drawing paper that has been divided into thirds. The first person draws the head of a "Grablin." The second person draws the "middle stuff," and the third person draws the legs and feet. (A "Grablin" is a Halloween character that tries to steal candy from trick-or-treaters.) After drawing the "Grablin," the team should color it. Then, each member of the team should write two sentences that describe "Grablin" characteristics. (What does it eat? Where does it live? When is it seen? How does it behave?)

Curriculum Integration
Challenge the students to design a goblin trap. Have the class illustrate and describe the trap.

Visuals
- Create large pictures of Dorrie and the goblin to put on display.

HARRIET'S HALLOWEEN CANDY

by Nancy Carlson

Synopsis
Harriet learns a valuable lesson about sharing.

Vocabulary
1. guilty
2. organized

Writing Activity
Instruct each student to write the name *Harriet* in large "bubble" letters on a sheet of drawing paper. Have the students fill in Harriet's name with as many words as they can think of that describe people they know. (The students may also draw pictures of Harriet that depict some of the descriptive words they have chosen.)

Curriculum Integration
Have the students create tagboard masks of Harriet and Walt to wear in short, original plays. Let the students write the dialogue!

Visuals
- Share an assortment of Halloween candy with the class.

THE HALLOWEEN PUMPKIN SMASHER

by Judith St. George

Synopsis
(This is a chapter book which may be read in three separate sittings.)

Join Mary Grace Potts and her make-believe friend as they attempt to solve the mystery of who is smashing all of the pumpkins on Grove Street. The solution to the mystery may surprise the reader.

Vocabulary

Chapter 1	Chapter 2	Chapter 3
1. cloak	1. belfry	1. canvas
2. gables	2. corn silk	2. fender
3. hedge	3. laurel bush	3. fumes
4. parlor	4. strap	4. hitching post
5. root cellar	5. woodshed	5. horsewhip
6. swooped		6. touring car
7. weather vane		

Writing Activity
Do not read the final page of the story. Ask the students to draw a picture of the pumpkin smasher and to write the ending of the story. (Note: Stop reading after this line on page 45: "I could be kind, too.")

Students will delight in creating and writing about their own imaginary friends.

Curriculum Integration
Make apple butter to spread on crackers.

1 cup applesauce	1 tsp. nutmeg
1/4 cup butter	1/3 cup sugar
1 tsp. cinnamon	

Boil the ingredients until the mixture darkens.

Visuals
- pictures of all kinds of pumpkins — smashed and whole

HUMBUG WITCH

by Lorna Balian

Synopsis
Children will enjoy the mysterious costume charade of the lovely leading character in this delightful holiday book.

Vocabulary
1. jiggle
2. potion
3. shawl
4. stringy
5. sturdy

Writing Activity
Guide the students in making original responses to this statement: If you could "play a trick" on your family and friends at Halloween by becoming anything you like, what would you be? Ask the students to draw their "costumes."

Encourage the students to "conjure up" their own recipes for a magic potion. Have each student explain what he or she would like the potion to do.

Curriculum Integration
Help the students develop thinking skills by asking them to respond to these questions:

If present-day Halloween "symbols" no longer existed, what new Halloween symbols would you choose to create? Instead of witches, bats, pumpkins and ghosts, what symbols would you like to represent Halloween? Explain why you have made each choice. Draw and color your symbols.

Visuals
• Create a felt-board Humbug Witch that you can assemble and disassemble as the story proceeds.

THE TEENY-TINY WOMAN

by Paul Galdone

Synopsis
The teeny-tiny woman from the teeny-tiny house in the teeny-tiny village finds a teeny-tiny bone that gives her more than a teeny-tiny scare.

Vocabulary
1. bonnet
2. teeny-tiny

Writing Activity
Point out to the students that when Paul Galdone animated the cupboard in the story, he began to see faces in many of his illustrations. (Check the graveyard fence and gate and the staircase railing.)

Every student will delight in creating a story scene that contains an inconspicuous face. Each student should write a couple of sentences to tell how the face would become part of the story. (Older students may be able to elaborate considerably on the original story.)

Another choice for a follow-up activity would be to encourage the students to write story endings that could have happened if the teeny-tiny woman had said, "Take it!" It is important for the students to illustrate their new endings.

Curriculum Integration
The students may create interesting teeny-tiny Halloween scenes by making shoe-box dioramas.

Visuals
• a small chicken bone and a box decorated like the cupboard

THE VANISHING PUMPKIN

by Tony Johnston

Synopsis
Where could a 700-year-old woman and an 800-year-old man go to find their missing pumpkin? Follow along on their travels and solve the pumpkin mystery.

Vocabulary
1. croaked
2. ghoul
3. rapscallion
4. reminds
5. snitched
6. varmint
7. wizard

Writing Activity
Have the class respond to the following questions:

> If the old woman and the old man had not found their pumpkin, what could they have substituted for their pie? What are the other choices that the man and the woman could have made if the pumpkin had not been found? How would the ending to the story change?

Brainstorm a list of possible uses for a pumpkin. Have each student cut out a pumpkin pattern (page 71) and illustrate one use on the pumpkin. Hang the pumpkins from the ceiling or display them on a bulletin board or wall.

Curriculum Integration
Have each student formulate a recipe for something (other than pumpkin pie) that requires pumpkin. Instruct the students to write their "Pumpkin, Other-than-Pumpkin-Pie" recipes on recipe cards.

Ask these questions: What are some interesting facts about pumpkins?

How did pumpkins become part of the Halloween celebration?

Visuals
• pumpkins

THE BOOK OF PIGERICKS
by Arnold Lobel

Synopsis
An aging pig writes limericks about other pigs from various places.

Vocabulary
1. anguish	6. despair	11. entrapped	16. pranced
2. assailed	7. despised	12. frock	17. tidbits
3. botanical	8. discontent	13. grieved	18. uncouth
4. commotion	9. eiderdown	14. ladle	19. vague
5. concealing	10. enrapt	15. passions	

Writing Activity
Although writing limericks can be quite complex for primary children, using a limerick pattern can help to simplify the process of creating a successful product. Using the form provided, students may create "pigericks" about pigs from towns or cities with which they are familiar. (See the following page.) Have the students illustrate their poems.

Curriculum Integration
Students can sharpen their map skills by finding the location of each pig's home. Have the students draw maps and chart the journey from one home to another. Students may approximate mileage from one home to another and create original math problems using this information.

Visuals
- pictures of pigs
- Lobel's illustrations

Name _____

LIMERICK PATTERN

In a limerick, lines 1, 2, and 5 rhyme.
Lines 3 and 4 also rhyme.

EXAMPLE:
(1)   There once was a teacher named *Cook*,
(2)   Who loved to read many a *book*,
(3)   Though she tried to cut *back*,
(4)   It was hard to be *slack*,
(5)   She'd end up just taking a *look*.

Oftentimes a limerick will begin with "there once was."
Try writing a limerick following this pattern:

(1) There once was _____ ,

(2) Who _____ ,

(3) _____ ,

(4) _____ ,

(5) _____ .

Illustrate your limerick here:

CAN I KEEP HIM?

by Steven Kellogg

Synopsis
Arnold suggests several pets to his mother because he is lonely and looking for a playmate. His mother seems to have a good excuse for not accepting any of them.

Vocabulary
1. allergic
2. annoy
3. appetite
4. buck
5. disagreeable
6. enormous
7. fawn
8. shed
10. untidy
11. wandering

Writing Activity
Discuss this question: If you could have any pet in the world, what kind of pet would you choose? Have the students illustrate their chosen pets and tell how they would convince their moms that they should keep their pets.

Curriculum Integration
Arnold wanted a dinosaur for a pet. Have the students research to find out about another extinct animal. Students should find answers for these questions:

1. Where did the animal live?
2. What did the animal look like? (Describe and sketch it.)
3. Why did the animal become extinct?

Visuals
• Examine Kellogg's illustrations for details and discuss aspects of a good illustration.

CHESTER THE WORLDLY PIG

by Bill Peet

Synopsis
Follow the adventures of Chester, an unsatisfied pig who longs to perform with the circus, as his road to success is fraught with near-fatal events.

Vocabulary
1. aimlessly
2. amazement
3. canvas
4. cumbersome
5. dauntless
6. despair
7. desperation
8. dingy
9. dreary
10. elegant
11. embankment
12. feat
13. ferocious
14. frantically
15. furious
16. horrified
17. mastered
18. outlandish
19. plume
20. revolving
21. roustabouts
22. rumbled
23. snout
24. spry
25. strides
26. tattered
27. trough

Writing Activity
When a showoff is called a ham, the word ham is being used as a figure of speech. Have each student brainstorm for a list of figures of speech. After the list has been compiled, let each student illustrate his or her favorite figure of speech both literally and as it is meant to be interpreted. The student should write the figure of speech and what it means to him or her beneath the picture.

Curriculum Integration
Conduct research on the commercial uses for pigs. (Examples: ham, footballs, etc.)

Visuals
- pictures of pigs
- Bill Peet's illustrations

THE DAY JIMMY'S BOA ATE THE WASH

by Trinka Hakes Noble

Synopsis
A "boring and kind of dull" class trip to the farm turns into an exciting adventure in which pigs eat lunches on school buses and boa constrictors create egg fights.

Vocabulary
1. boa constrictor
2. squawking

Writing Activity
A boa constrictor is a rather unusual pet. Some mothers may not appreciate having a pet of this nature around the house. Each student should select an unusual animal to draw. Then the student should prepare an argument to convince Mom or Dad that the pet should be permitted to stay. (A panel of student "parents" may be selected to choose the most convincing arguments.)

Curriculum Integration
Students may wish to create an animal puppet and act out another misadventure that could have happened "the day Jimmy's boa ate the wash."

Visuals
- pictures of boa constrictors
- Kellogg's illustrations

GREGORY THE TERRIBLE EATER

by Mitchell Sharmat

Synopsis
Gregory the goat has a terrible problem — he does not like eating junk food. He prefers fruits and vegetables for a nutritious diet. Mother and father goat finally help him find "balanced" meals.

Vocabulary
1. average
2. barber pole
3. condition
4. develop
5. munching
6. revolting
7. terrible

Writing Activity
Have the students use the *"Create A New Product"* student page to create a new food product that would appeal to both Gregory and his parents. (Provide canned food labels for the students to examine.)

Curriculum Integration
Allow the students to find out more about the four food groups. Then have the students create a menu for a day of healthy meals.

Visuals
- an example of junk food
- an example of the "junk food" Gregory refused to eat

CREATE A NEW PRODUCT

Think of a food product that would appeal to both Gregory and his parents.

Create a label for the can in which the food would be packaged.

The label should contain these things:

1. product name
2. manufacturer's name
3. number of calories per serving
4. list of ingredients
5. information about the product's quality
6. reason(s) why the product should be purchased

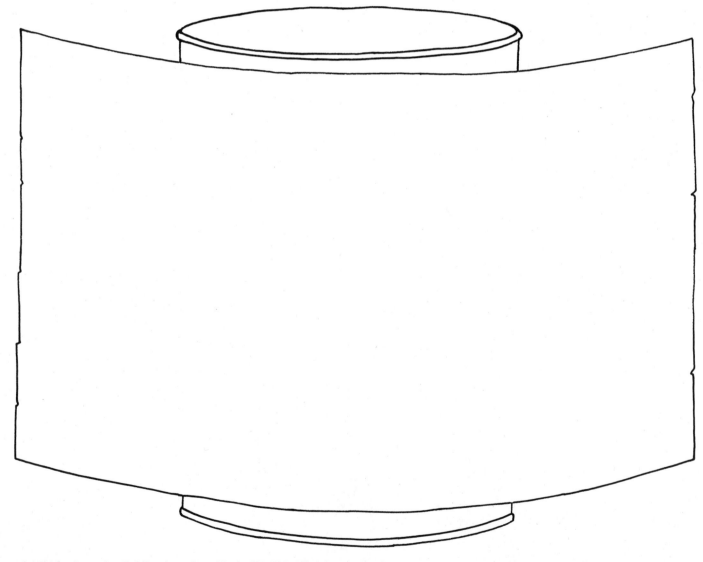

I WILL NOT GO TO MARKET TODAY

by Harry Allard

Synopsis
If you have ever decided to "wait until tomorrow" to do something, you will be able to identify with Allard's rib-tickling tale!

Vocabulary
1. blizzard
2. hurricane
3. market
4. raging
5. stile

Writing Activity
Fenimore B. Buttercrunch had many excuses why he could not go to market. Have the students invent and illustrate an excuse that Fenimore did not use.

Have the students develop their own lists of excuses for things that they usually "put off" until later. Instruct the students to illustrate these excuses and combine them to create a small book.

Example:
I cannot practice the piano now because _____ .
On the way to begin my homework, I got sidetracked by _____
_____ .

Curriculum Integration
Discuss how marketing has changed over the last 50 years. Brainstorm the pros and cons of the small market versus the large-scale warehouse grocery store of today.

Visuals
- Let the class enjoy jam and toast and tea.
- Show Marshall's illustrations.

LOUANNE PIG
IN THE PERFECT FAMILY

by Nancy Carlson

Synopsis
Louanne Pig, an only child, discovers that the grass is not necessarily greener on the other side of the fence when she goes to stay with George for the weekend. George has a "perfect" family of twelve.

Vocabulary
1. adopting
2. clang
3. discovery
4. ignore
5. perfect

Writing Activity
Discuss the value of calling cards and what kind of information they contain. (Share samples with the class if you can.) Have each student design a calling card for a character in the story (see the *"Calling Cards"* student page).

Curriculum Integration
Instruct the students to draw pictures of their perfect families and tell what makes their families "perfect."

Visuals
- Show the class Nancy Carlson's illustrations. Help the students draw simple pigs or bunnies patterned after the ones in Carlson's book.

CALLING CARDS

Design a calling card for a character in the story.

THE MAGNIFICENT MOO
by Victoria Forrester

Synopsis
The cow decides that she is unhappy with her moo and trades it with another animal who then trades the moo with another animal, and so forth, until finally the moo comes full circle to be "reunited" with the cow.

Vocabulary
1. amazement
2. exception
3. magnificent
4. marvelous
5. nasturtiums
6. pasture
7. pollen
8. splendid
9. twitched

Writing Activity
Allow each student to create another character to "insert" into the chain of events in the story. Students should create their characters on paper and write the parts of the story that they wish to have inserted. Prepare a flannel board presentation and ask the students to create felt representations of their characters. (Cut out a student's paper drawing and glue it to felt.) Then the students may practice telling their stories in small groups.

Curriculum Integration
Have the students brainstorm a list of animals and their sounds.

Visuals
- Create a flannel board presentation.

PIG PIG GOES TO CAMP

by David McPhail

Synopsis

Pig Pig's mother struggles each year trying to persuade him to go to camp. When Pig Pig finally decides to go to Camp Wildhog, he discovers that he loves it. Camp loves him, too, until he becomes too popular.

Vocabulary

1. assigned
2. boarded
3. conduct
4. decided
5. director
6. miserable
7. participated
8. prepared

Writing Activity

Students can engage in creative problem solving as they imagine themselves to be director of Camp Wildhog. Have the students illustrate their answers to this question: If the option of sending Pig Pig home had not been available, how could you as camp director have solved the frog problem to everyone's satisfaction?

Problem Solving Steps

1. State problem
2. List facts
3. List necessary information
4. State alternatives
5. List criteria
6. Give solution
7. Convince others of the worth of the solution

Curriculum Integration

Purchase three copies of the paperback edition of this book. Cut up two copies and mount the pictures on tagboard. If possible, laminate these pictures and place them in a center for students to use in sequencing. As the students practice sequencing, they also can practice oral storytelling skills.

Visuals

- the book's illustrations

THE STORY OF FERDINAND

by Munro Leaf

Synopsis
This book is truly a children's classic. It is the story of a young bull who wishes to sit and smell the flowers rather than fight.

Vocabulary
1. banderilleros
2. cork tree
3. fierce
4. Madrid
5. matador
6. pasture
7. picadores
8. snort
9. Spain

Writing Activity
Help the students examine more closely the issues involved in bull-fighting. Then ask them to take a position on the issues.

1. Bulls should not be killed for sport because _____ .
2. Bull fights should be allowed to continue as sporting events because _____ .

Instruct the students to design posters in support of the positions they have taken. (This would be a good time to discuss persuasive advertising.)

Curriculum Integration
Have the students conduct research on the history of bullfighting. Some questions students may wish to answer are as follows:
1. When did bullfighting begin?
2. Where did bullfighting originate?

Visuals
- other stories about bullfighting
- pictures of bulls and bullfighters

ARTHUR'S THANKSGIVING

by Marc Brown

Synopsis
Arthur is elected to direct the Thanksgiving play for the class. A problem develops when no one will volunteer to be the turkey. A hilarious solution to the problem will surprise the reader.

Vocabulary
1. appointment	6. desperate	11. glamorous	16. rejoicing
2. auditorium	7. direct	12. narrator	17. smooth
3. breath	8. disaster	13. outfit	18. symbol
4. complained	9. entire	14. performance	19. turkeys
5. curtain	10. explained		

Writing Activity
Arthur created posters to display in the cafeteria which advertised the role of a turkey in the school play. Instruct each student to write an advertisement for a job or a product. Discuss the skill of putting your thoughts into a few words. Remind the students to make their products or jobs sound appealing to the reader. (Illustrations would help.) Compile the students' ads in a mini-newspaper for their enjoyment. Examples from newspapers will help the students understand advertising. Encourage the students to bring their favorite ads from home.

Curriculum Integration
Decorate a large poster board with a picture of a turkey. Cut out a hole for a student's face. Let the students pose for individual turkey photos (be sure to have a camera handy!).

Visuals
- newspapers
- additional books by Marc Brown

CRANBERRY THANKSGIVING

by Wende and Harry Devlin

Synopsis
Maggie and her grandmother invite two very special guests for Thanksgiving dinner. Grandmother dislikes Mr. Whiskers until he saves her secret recipe from disappearing. (The secret recipe for cranberry bread is included in the story.)

Vocabulary
1.	bog	5.	edge	9.	lavender	13.	sniffle
2.	curtains	6.	effort	10.	recipe	14.	starch
3.	delicious	7.	encourage	11.	scuffle	15.	tender
4.	disgrace	8.	exquisite	12.	shutters	16.	whiskers

Writing Activity
Grandmother was famous for her cranberry bread recipe. Let the students discuss their favorite foods. Make a graph to illustrate their favorites. When Maggie tasted cranberry bread, she always thought of her grandmother. Many foods remind people of other people, special places, or experiences. Discuss these ideas with the class. Following the discussion about food, assist the students in writing a project titled "Food For Thought." Have each student list many different items of food and tell what experiences each food brings to mind.

Examples:
Apples make me think of going to the orchard with my family.
Blueberries make me think of going to my Grandmother's house.
Popcorn makes me think of going to the movies.

Curriculum Integration
Bake Grandmother's famous cranberry bread. (Directions are in the back of the book.)

Visuals
- a map of the U.S. with the New England states marked
- a recipe book for browsing

IT'S THANKSGIVING

by Jack Prelutsky

Synopsis
This delightful book contains lighthearted poetry covering every aspect of Thanksgiving — from the turkey to the traditional football game.

Vocabulary
1. anticipate	5. cozy	9. jubilant	13. murals
2. bountiful	6. drizzling	10. luscious	14. perky
3. bungled	7. hover	11. maize	15. shreds
4. bustles	8. interception	12. mammoth	16. wattle

Writing Activity
(Depending upon the age of the students, this project may require some advance preparation.) Have the students create Thanksgiving riddles. They should follow these steps:
1. Choose a Thanksgiving subject (turkey, pumpkin pie, family, overeating, etc.).
2. Write four clues about the subject on the *"What Am I?"* student page.
3. Cut open the door on the *"What Am I?"* student page. (Cut only on the dotted lines.)
4. Draw a picture of the subject of your riddle on another sheet of paper. Glue the picture behind the door so that when the door opens the answer to the riddle will be revealed.

Curriculum Integration
Let the students try original cartooning. Ask each student to investigate the origins of Thanksgiving. After finishing the investigation, each student should create an original cartoon character that could present the collected information through the comic strip format.

(Provide the students with examples of comic strips and pages of comic strip "windows.")

Visuals
- Thanksgiving pictures
- Thanksgiving memorabilia

WHAT AM I?

Choose a Thanksgiving subject.
Write four clues about the subject.

Cut the door along the dotted lines.
Draw a picture of your subject on another sheet of paper.
Glue the picture behind the door to "answer" the riddle.

ONE TERRIFIC THANKSGIVING

by Marjorie Weinman Sharmat

Synopsis

Irving Morris Bear has a passion for food. After doing his Thanksgiving grocery shopping, he asks his friends to hide his food from him so that it will be safe for Thanksgiving Day. When he changes his mind and wants it back, chaos takes over and teaches him a lesson.

Vocabulary

1. arrived	5. feast	8. imagination	11. official
2. depend	6. goodness	9. immediately	12. overturned
3. desperate	7. guardian	10. knuckle under	13. shrugged
4. examined			

Writing Activity

Instruct each student to compose a letter of advice to Irving Morris Bear (as though he or she were Morris Bear's doctor). Students could write about the effects of overindulgence, high cholesterol, excessive sugar in the diet, etc. (Students may choose to be dentists sending letters of advice, also.) Encourage the students to research health risks related to improper eating.

Curriculum Integration

Irving Morris Bear wears a T-shirt proclaiming "I ♡ food."

Have the students design a more appropriate T-shirt to help Irving Morris Bear take his mind off of food. Students may use fabric, crayons and old T-shirts to actually reproduce their designs.

Visuals

- Share stuffed bears and munchy marshmallows.

ONE TOUGH TURKEY

by Steven Kroll

Synopsis
In this story, the reader "hears" about the Thanksgiving celebration from the turkeys in a slapstick manner. The turkeys do hilarious things to the Pilgrims when the Pilgrims try to capture them for Thanksgiving Day dinner.

Vocabulary

1. bunch	6. hoisted	10. shoulder
2. captain	7. musket	11. stunned
3. exact	8. Pilgrims	12. surprise
4. explained	9. pursuit	13. trampled
5. gesture		

Writing Activity
The author tells the story from the turkey's point of view. Discuss the fact that everyone has an opinion and sees things a little differently. Show examples of "point of view" articles from a newspaper. Instruct each student to write a paragraph from an object's or another person's point of view. The object may take on human qualities for this activity. Some suggestions include:

- How the bus feels when children ride it to school
- A library book's point of view when someone reads it
- An airplane's point of view when you take a trip in it
- A car's point of view when a family travels in it

Curriculum Integration
Have the class compare the wild turkey to the domestic turkey by creating a poster detailing the birds' differences.

Visuals
- additional books by Steven Kroll
- point-of-view newspaper articles

SOMETIMES IT'S TURKEY, SOMETIMES IT'S FEATHERS

by Lorna Balian

Synopsis
Mrs. Gumm finds an egg while hunting for mushrooms. The egg hatches into a spectacular turkey that she grows to love.

Vocabulary
1. cornmeal	4. genuine	7. mushrooms	10. strawberries
2. flannel	5. hatch	8. plenty	11. tender
3. freckles	6. imagine	9. plump	12. treasure

Writing Activity
Instruct the students to write and illustrate a time line for the story. (The time line will run from May to November.) Give the students very long strips of paper — approximately 96 inches in length. Let the students use rulers to mark off seven sections on their strips of paper. They should then illustrate the growth of the turkey and "tell" the story in sentences.

Curriculum Integration
Allow each child to dip a hard-boiled egg in dye and create speckles with glitter.

Research information about real turkeys to find answers to these questions:
Where can wild turkeys be found?
How do turkey farms operate?
What is the average price of a turkey in a local grocery store?

Visuals
- If possible, display pictures of turkeys during various stages of their growth.

THANKSGIVING AT THE TAPPLETON'S

by Eileen Spinelli

Synopsis
The turkey mysteriously slips through the door of the Tappleton home before the Thanksgiving dinner occurs. To the surprise of everyone, the Tappleton family has a wonderful holiday.

Vocabulary
1. aluminum	5. liverwurst	9. rhubarb	12. sneeze
2. certain	6. refrigerator	10. skid	13. stomach
3. empty	7. remark	11. slithered	14. trimmings
4. groan	8. replied		

Writing Activity
Humor is important as a survival skill for all people. Discuss how humor helped the Tappletons survive a bad situation. After the discussion, let the students write favorite jokes for the class, or have them write about funny situations they have experienced. Compile a class joke book for display.

Curriculum Integration
Let the students make original turkeys using potatoes for the bodies and artificial feathers! Colored construction paper can provide additional details.

Visuals
- joke books

THANKSGIVING DAY

by Gail Gibbons

Synopsis
A historic time line about the first Thanksgiving's origins and its traditions is presented in a colorful and unique manner. Gail Gibbons provides the reader with a view of the current Thanksgiving traditions which enables one to compare the past and present.

Vocabulary
1.	arrived	4.	decorated	7.	friends	10.	harvest
2.	cornstalks	5.	feast	8.	gathered	11.	pumpkins
3.	cranberry	6.	finally	9.	gourds	12.	squash

Writing Activity
Instruct each student to develop a comparison chart to illustrate Thanksgivings of long ago and Thanksgivings of today.

Curriculum Integration
The illustrations are clear and distinctive examples of the artistic use of foreground, middleground, and background. Examine the illustrations and allow the students to create pictures using three components.

Visuals
- Research books and materials about boats, Native Americans, and the Pilgrims.
- Display cornstalk dolls to demonstrate the use of natural materials for art.

THINGS TO MAKE AND DO FOR THANKSGIVING

by Lorinda Bryan Cauley

Synopsis

Ideas for recipes, jokes, riddles, crafts, and a sample map outlining the history of the first Thanksgiving are attractively illustrated to excite the young reader. The many ideas presented will be a starting point for children to create.

Vocabulary

1. animals
2. center
3. design
4. dessert
5. different
6. enough
7. feather
8. Indians
9. molasses
10. nutmeg
11. Pilgrims
12. puppet
13. radishes
14. remove
15. riddles
16. roasted
17. sprouts
18. weather
19. yogurt

Writing Activity

Ask the students to follow these directions to create personal Thanksgiving "Make and Do" booklets:

1. Design a cover using leaf rubbings (see pages 14 and 15 in the book).
2. Write an original recipe for a Thanksgiving meal or dessert.
3. Write a Thanksgiving riddle (see the examples on pages 42 and 43 in the book).
4. Illustrate Indian picture writing as described in the book on pages 44 and 45.

Curriculum Integration

Make an apple turkey statue as directed on page 17 in the book.
Supplies:

apple	12 cranberries
8 toothpicks	lettuce leaf
a large marshmallow	10 raisins
plate	scissors

Visuals

- Indian artifacts
- books related to Thanksgiving and Native Americans

A CHOCOLATE MOOSE
FOR DINNER

by Fred Gwynne

Synopsis
Fred Gwynne brings humor to the oddities our imaginations can "drum up" when we immerse ourselves in the English language — homonyms to delight everyone's funny bone!

Vocabulary
1. arms race
2. chocolate moose
3. Dali
4. gorilla war
5. "on the lam"
6. sculling
7. toasted
8. undertow

Writing Activity
Students can create their own "hilarious homonyms" by brainstorming words and phrases that can be used in more than one way. (Discuss what the term homonym means.)

After choosing one pair of homonyms or one picturesque "figure of speech," each student should illustrate the words. Students might enjoy making watercolor overlays of their pictures to place on top of their boldy printed phrases.

Curriculum Integration
Let the students enjoy creating a chocolate mousse using this recipe:
   1 stick margarine
   3/4 cup sugar
   1 tsp. vanilla
   2 eggs
   1 square unsweetened baking
      chocolate

Cream butter and sugar; add melted chocolate and vanilla. Add 1 egg. Beat five minutes on medium speed. Add second egg and beat five minutes. Chill two hours and serve.

Visuals
● a chocolate candy moose
● homonym cards

ALEXANDER AND THE WIND-UP MOUSE

by Leo Lionni

Synopsis

Alexander shares the trials and tribulations of being a real mouse with Willy, his wind-up toy mouse friend. A lizard's magic wish makes it possible for Alexander and Willy to live happily ever after.

Vocabulary

1. alas	4. hide-out	7. ordinary	10. quivering
2. baseboard	5. in vain	8. pantry	11. wooly
3. envy	6. mysteriously	9. precious	

Writing Activity

Help the students rewrite the ending of the story by changing Alexander's wish. Alexander stays with his original idea and has the lizard turn him into a wind-up mouse. How would the new story end?

Students will have fun creating mouse-size tales. Each student can write a mouse mini-adventure to place in the class mouse-size book. Students should illustrate their stories.

Curriculum Integration

Lionni created uniquely beautiful illustrations for his book without drawing. Students can, too! Allow the students to use various types of paper (tissue, construction, wallpaper, wrapping paper, etc.) to recreate their favorite sections of the story. (Scissors may or may not be used.)

Visuals

- a wind-up toy mouse
- Lionni's illustrations

ANIMALS SHOULD DEFINITELY NOT WEAR CLOTHING

by Judi Barrett

Synopsis
Whether it be fur, feathers, or skin of assorted types, animals have the best "clothing" of all. As this book illustrates, wearing "people clothes" might cause animals to have a world of trouble.

Vocabulary
1. disastrous
2. embarrassing
3. manage
4. opossums
5. porcupine
6. unnecessary

Writing Activity
Students can develop their own books about someone or something who should definitely not do something.

Example:
Animals should definitely not chew gum.

Later, let students expand their ideas to make individually-illustrated books.

Curriculum Integration
Instruct each student to choose an animal that lives in the wild and to conduct research about its naturally protective clothing. Ask students to respond to this question: If the animal's natural hide were changed, how would it affect the animal's life?

Visuals
- pictures of animals (from the book) in their natural habitats
- Barrett's illustrations

ARTHUR'S NOSE

by Marc Brown

Synopsis
Arthur the aardvark doesn't like his nose. It is too large, too unusual, and too "stuffed up"! However, Arthur's search for a new nose leads him to a surprising decision.

Vocabulary
1. aardvark
2. armadillo
3. nuisance
4. toucan

Writing Activity
Guide the students in answering the following questions and then have the students illustrate their answers.

If I could change one thing about the way I look, I would change _____ because _____ .

If I could change Arthur's nose, I would choose a _____ nose for him because _____ _____ .

Curriculum Integration
Allow the students to create aardvark paper plate puppets. The noses on the puppets should be those of other animals! Allow the students to use their puppets to "act out" new endings for the story.

Visuals
- pictures of aardvarks
- Brown's humorous illustrations

BEAR SHADOW

by Frank Asch

Synopsis

Frank Asch's bear returns. This time he has a problem. His shadow keeps scaring the fish he is about to catch.

Vocabulary

1. exclaimed
2. pride
3. shadow

Writing Activity

Students will delight in thinking of another way that the bear could have gotten rid of his shadow. Ask the students to illustrate their ideas.

Curriculum Integration

Let the class experiment with making different kinds of shadow puppets. Use an overhead projector or filmstrip projector as the light source. Allow small groups of students to create new story characters who are merely shadows. Students also may choose to write adventures for their shadow creations.

Visuals

- Create shadows on the wall.
- Bring a big stuffed bear to class for the students to sit with as the story is read.

BIG BAD BRUCE

by Bill Peet

Synopsis
Big Bad Bruce is a bully of a bear and the terror of the forest until he incurs the ire of Roxy the Witch. Although Roxy can't completely change this bothersome bear, she greatly diminishes the trouble that he can cause.

Vocabulary
1. aroma
2. blunder
3. brambles
4. canyon
5. crafty
6. desperation
7. diminish
8. drowsy
9. dwindled
10. frantic
11. gape
12. gradually
13. grubs
14. "hatched a plot"
15. headlong
16. lummox
17. pell-mell
18. prowl
19. raucous
20. scruff
21. scurried
22. shrivel
23. slinky
24. smithereens
25. snatched
26. soggy
27. thicket
28. underbrush
29. weary

Writing Activity
Students should brainstorm for a list of words or phrases having "bear" at the core or root such as unbearable, bearing, bear down, bear hug, bearer, etc.

After choosing a favorite word, each student should draw a character who depicts in some way the chosen word. Then the student should write a sentence or two about the character traits of this newly invented character.

Or, stop reading the story on page 13. At that point discuss "plot" with the students. Ask the students to put themselves into the witch's spot and think about what kind of a plot they would hatch to end the antics of the bothersome bear. Have the students complete the story and share their endings with the class.

they can for the vocabulary words listed above.

Curriculum Integration
Have the students use a thesaurus or dictionary to find as many similes as

Visuals
- pictures of bears
- Bill Peet's illustrations

HELGA HIGH-UP

by Marjorie Sharmat

Synopsis
Helga is unhappy with her considerable height, even though she is a giraffe. When her height helps her perform a heroic deed, she discovers how wonderful it is to be exactly who she is.

Vocabulary
1. "crick in the neck"
2. example
3. gasped
4. headfirst
5. hero
6. perfect
7. posture
8. practiced
9. presently
10. shrink
11. slumped
12. yanked

Writing Activity
Direct the students to forecast the future for Helga and the other story characters by writing fortune cookie predictions for each of them.

Make brown paper fortune cookies. Fold the cookies in half and insert fortune strips. Have each child create three or four fortune cookies. Let the students exchange cookies in small groups and guess to whom the fortunes might apply. Characters for whom they may write fortunes should include:
1. Helga
2. the robber lion
3. the raccoon
4. the cow
5. Ms. Rabbit
6. Ralston
7. Helga's mom or dad

   Example: (for tiger) You will be going on a long trip. Be sure to pack your striped pajamas.

Curriculum Integration
Brainstorm for measures that should be taken in order to prevent crimes. Examine a newspaper to see how many stories concern crime. Ask the students to address the question of why crime occurs.

Visuals
- Let the students eat fortune cookies as you read the story.

HUBERT'S HAIR-RAISING ADVENTURE

by Bill Peet

Synopsis

Peet tells in rhyme the story of Hubert, a vain lion whose mane goes up in flame. Through the magic powers of crocodile tears, the bald head sprouts more mane than needed or wanted. Eventually, Hubert's vanity is restored.

Vocabulary

1. absurd	14. disgust	27. ignited	39. restored
2. avoid	15. dread	28. lopped	40. riot
3. boulder	16. drifting	29. lumbered	41. shed
4. broadcast	17. elegant	30. lunged	42. smug
5. bungle	18. emeralds	31. managed	43. special
6. conceit	19. fake	32. mane	44. spied
7. confess	20. fantastic	33. moaned	45. spiraled
8. consider	21. fetch	34. obvious	46. sprout
9. cure	22. forged	35. perched	47. stubbles
10. delightful	23. gossip	36. progressed	48. style
11. departed	24. guffaws	37. recline	49. thrashed
12. diminished	25. hasty	38. regret	50. vain
13. disgrace	26. haughty		

Writing Activity

This activity should take place before the story is read. Bill Peet uses an outstanding array of words when creating his stories. Write each vocabulary word on an index card and have each student draw two cards out of a hat. The student must then use each word in a sentence and write the sentences on separate dictionary entry pages. (Each student should have access to the dictionary.) Make copies of all of the entries and present each child with his or her own copy of "Hubert's Dictionary" (page 105 is the booklet cover; page 106 is the dictionary entry page).

Curriculum Integration

Bill Peet worked for many years as a cartoon artist and writer. Ask the

students to find out more about how cartoons are created. Then have the students design their own cartoon characters.

Visuals

- other books by Bill Peet

HUBERT'S DICTIONARY

Name:_____

Word Definition:

Sentence:

Illustration:

IF YOU GIVE A MOUSE A COOKIE

by Laura Joffe Numeroff

Synopsis
In a circular chain of events, a mouse is given a cookie. Of course, he then needs a glass of milk which in turns prompts him to need a napkin, etc. The chain continues until the mouse finds himself needing another cookie.

Vocabulary
1. mustache
2. nail scissors
3. probably

Writing Activity
Ask each student to choose an additional item that the mouse could request and to determine its placement in the story. Then have the student draw an illustration for the story change. (You may choose to make a flannel board pattern and to allow the students to tell the story with their newly created additions.)

Curriculum Integration
Help the class make a batch of cookies!

Investigate to find out what kinds of foods mice living in the wild really eat.

Visuals
- Patterns are provided for a flannel board presentation.
- Eat cookies after the story.

FLANNEL BOARD PATTERNS

IT WASN'T MY FAULT

by Helen Lester

Synopsis
Murdley Gurdson tries to find out whose fault it is that an egg has landed on his head. He finally comes to the conclusion that it may be his own fault.

Vocabulary
1. aardvark
2. confessed
3. fault
4. pygmy hippo
5. valuable

Writing Activity
Murdley Gurdson's egg adventure is a great deal like "a Rube Goldberg" — one thing causes a chain reaction of complications which produces a simple result in a complicated way. Show the students some examples of Rube Goldbergs. Then ask the students to create Goldberg-type inventions by illustrating the chain of events. Have the students write brief descriptions of how their inventions work.

Curriculum Integration
Let the students create a scrambled egg sampler. Students may decide to add additional ingredients such as ham, cheese, mushrooms, onions, etc. Enjoy the eggs as you read another "eggs-tra" special book!

Visuals
- different kinds of eggs
- the book's illustrations

NOSEY MRS. RAT

by Jeffrey Allen

Synopsis
Nosey Mrs. Rat is the bothersome neighborhood snoop who overhears and sees everything. She finally meets her match in a hilarious adventure with Brewster Blackstone.

Vocabulary
1. amusing	7. engaged	13. occasions	18. private
2. attracted	8. expensive	14. peculiar	19. recognize
3. brand	9. humiliated	15. personally	20. scaled
4. concentrating	10. hysterics	16. poking around	21. shamelessly
5. confidential	11. miserable	17. prefer	22. solution
6. disguise	12. nosiest		

Writing Activity
The students will need large (4" x 9") vocabulary cards (write each vocabulary word and its definition on a card). Let each student choose two vocabulary word cards and draw a character or characters from the story on each card in a manner which illustrates the word.

Example:

Nosiest

A person who minds everyone else's business is one of the nosiest people there is.

Curriculum Integration
Brainstorm interesting things about which the students would like to know more. Discuss the students' responses.

Visuals
- Marshall's humorous illustrations

PELICAN

by Brian Wildsmith

Synopsis
Paul finds an egg that is different from any that he has ever seen. The pelican that emerges creates mischief amidst Wildsmith's mysteriously changing settings and comes to be much loved by the boy and his family.

Vocabulary
1. damage
2. discovered
3. gleamed
4. gobbled
5. kingfisher
6. pelican
7. port
8. relieved
9. speckled
10. stroked
11. trout

Writing Activity
This book provides a wonderful opportunity for students to understand how the setting unfolds through pictures as well as the written word. Ask each student to imagine a setting for a story he or she could create. The setting should be detailed and filled with bright colors. Then have each student create a "hidden setting" picture using the format of Wildsmith's book.

Curriculum Integration
Have the students compose their own lists of differences between the pelican and the farm hen. Students should illustrate each difference.

Visuals
• the book's illustrations

TANGLES

by Nancy Polette

Synopsis

Tangles the lion hates his unmanageable mane. The zoo keeper tries a variety of remedies and Tangles muses about others, but a few little tangles finally calm the outraged and angry king.

Vocabulary

1. abundant
2. angered
3. constantly
4. contented
5. cosmopolitan
6. currying
7. dangerous
8. dehydrated
9. delight
10. dignity
11. disarray
12. reign
13. shining

Writing Activity

Have the students brainstorm a list of synonyms that could be used in a character development. Instruct the students to write brief character descriptions and to illustrate their newly developed characters.

Curriculum Integration

Students can create paper plate lions with curly construction paper manes to use in creating new Tangles tales.

Visuals

- a stuffed lion

ZOO DOINGS

by Jack Prelutsky

Synopsis
Animal verses from three of Jack Prelutsky's first books are gathered in one delightful volume.

Vocabulary
1. agility
2. audible
3. beacons
4. debonair
5. devour
6. dexterous
7. disinclined
8. domain
9. drafty
10. emerges
11. fleece
12. foe
13. gaggle
14. generate
15. hesitate
16. lopes
17. meek
18. multilingual
19. mynah bird
20. notion
21. obese
22. optical illusion
23. patter
24. ponders
25. prey
26. sloth
27. subterranean
28. trifle

Writing Activity
Have the students construct a zoo of nonexistent animals. Instruct the students to draw, color, and cut out the animals. A short, four-line verse (follow the AB, AB pattern) should be created to accompany each animal. Display the animals in zoo cages and attach the verses to the cages.

Curriculum Integration
Ask each student to discover three facts about an animal whose natural home is not the United States. Students can create clay models of their animals and write brief newspaper bulletins about the mysterious appearances of their animals in the United States. The animals' habitats should be discussed in the articles as well as speculation as to how the animals arrived in the United States.

Visuals
- pictures of animals mentioned in the book

ARTHUR'S CHRISTMAS

by Marc Brown

Synopsis

Arthur has a major problem deciding what present to give Santa. A hilarious adventure occurs as Arthur creates a wonderful meal for Santa.

Vocabulary

1. caroling
2. chimney
3. copied
4. drugstore
5. family
6. fudge
7. gloves
8. grouch
9. hundred
10. mittens
11. peppers
12. problem
13. remind
14. shopping

Writing Activity

Arthur uses a tongue twister in the story. Share tongue twisters with the class and have them create their own!

The meal that Arthur creates for Santa is enormous in size. Discuss what favorite foods the students would like to leave for Santa. Instruct each student to write a special note to Santa describing the meal he or she would like to leave for Santa on Christmas morning. The students should include reasons for their selections in their letters.

Curriculum Integration

Create Arthur posters advertising Marc Brown's books.

Visuals

- Display additional Arthur stories by Marc Brown.

BAH! HUMBUG?

by Lorna Balian

Synopsis
Margie's older brother, Arthur, tries to discourage her about Santa Claus' visit. The two children create a humorous trap for Santa Claus and little Margie is the only one who gets to see him.

Vocabulary

1. chimes	5. pajamas	9. trap
2. collecting	6. secret	10. worn
3. everything	7. skates	11. wrong
4. hanging	8. stockings	

Writing Activity
Margie will inspire young writers to develop personal letters to Santa Claus. Provide special stationery, envelopes, and stamps for the students.

Discuss phrases such as quiet as a mouse, tall as a giraffe, cold as ice, white as snow, etc. Make a list of other phrases as a group.

Discuss similes and their meanings. Ask the students to create original similes.

Curriculum Integration
A field trip to the post office would be an appropriate follow-up to this wonderful story.

Design a coffee bear. Ask each student to draw a bear and to spread glue and dried coffee grounds on the bear for texture. Details may be added with construction paper, fabric, ribbon, buttons, etc.

Visuals
- books about real and make-believe bears
- an appearance by Santa!

THE CHRISTMAS CAT

by Efner Tudor Holmes

Synopsis
The mysterious miracle of the Christmas cat leaves Nate and Jason trying to decide if it was Santa Claus or the kind grownup who surprised them on Christmas morning. The artistic presentation of the animals will warm the hearts of young readers.

Vocabulary
1. amazement
2. brilliant
3. confused
4. creatures
5. deserted
6. distant
7. emerge
8. exhausted
9. mangled
10. shiver
11. sympathetic

Writing Activity
Students will want to discuss the protection that animals need in winter following this story.

Ask each student to describe an animal using a riddle format.

Examples:
I have black and white stripes and a mane. What animal am I?

I am called a young colt at birth and I can be many colors. What animal am I?

I have a long neck and eat leaves from trees in Africa. What animal am I?

Curriculum Integration
Design bird feeders.

Materials: pine cones, peanut butter (thinned with oil so the birds won't get sick), sunflower seeds

Directions: Roll pine cones in a mixture of peanut butter and sunflower seeds. Attach strings to the cones and hang them in trees!

Visuals
- "animals in winter" books
- books about birds
- riddle books

THE COBWEB CHRISTMAS

by Shirley Climo

Synopsis
A little old German woman is a witness to some Christmas magic performed by curious spiders.

Vocabulary
1. canary
2. doze
3. glitter
4. marvelous
5. miracles
6. pane
7. pretzel
8. scrub
9. snore
10. speckled
11. spiders

Writing Activity
To begin the writing activity, give each student a large piece of drawing paper and have him or her draw the following spiders:

a huge spider	a spotted spider
a hairy spider	a smooth spider
a tiny spider	a striped spider
a brown, black and yellow spider	a pale, see-through spider

Ask the students to move like spiders in these ways:

creeping	crawling	sneaking
softly	scurrying	hurrying
quickly	lightly	zigging
zagging	weaving	wobbling

Create spider sentences using forms of the words listed above. The students may want to design spider books.

Curriculum Integration
Create construction paper spiders. Instruct the students to find three facts about spiders to write on their spiders.

Visuals
- a map of Germany (or a world map)
- pictures of spiders
- books about spiders

MADELINE'S CHRISTMAS

by Ludwig Bemelmans

Synopsis
Madeline calls upon a rug-selling magician to help her complete her daily chores. The twelve children celebrate an unusual Christmas as they fly about on magical rugs in a wondrous adventure.

Vocabulary
1. awful
2. creature
3. miserable
4. pause
5. stirring
6. straight

Writing Activity
Students will enjoy producing stories about the day the rug merchant brought magical rugs to their homes. Instruct each student to write a story about his or her adventures.

Curriculum Integration
Students can paint a mural depicting Madeline's Christmas. The mural should follow the sequence of the story.

Visuals
- Prepare a center featuring books by Ludwig Bemelmans.

THE POLAR EXPRESS

by Chris Van Allsburg

Synopsis
A young boy wakes up to the magical sound of the Polar Express train on Christmas Eve. As he arrives at the North Pole, the boy receives a special bell from Santa's sleigh.

Vocabulary
1. conductor	5. insisted	9. sped
2. distance	6. rustle	10. villages
3. factories	7. silent	11. whistle
4. harness	8. sleigh	12. wilderness

Writing Activity
Have the students complete the following statements:

If I knew that I could have any gift that I could imagine, I would want . . .

If I could take a train ride to any place in the world, I would like to see . . .

If I could ride with Santa on Christmas Eve, I would see . . .

Let the students share their responses with the group. Chris Van Allsburg's illustrations may inspire young artists to embellish their writings with original drawings.

Curriculum Integration
Create a North Pole city using the following materials:

papier-mâché mountains
cotton
cardboard house
small twigs
toy cars
a toy train for the Polar Express

Conduct research about trains or other transportation vehicles.

Visuals
- books about trains, planes, boats, etc.

BEGIN AT THE BEGINNING

by Amy Schwartz

Synopsis

Sara is given the honor of painting a wonderful picture for the second grade art show. She has only from the time she arrives home from school until bedtime to develop the creation, but she can't decide how to start.

Vocabulary

1. amazed	4. collapsed	7. immediately	10. rustle
2. appeared	5. crumpled	8. moaned	11. universe
3. chanted	6. depending	9. procrastination	

Writing Activity

Sara is a procrastinator. People sometimes procrastinate if a task they must do seems either too difficult or too dull.

Students should write brief stories in which they are the procrastinating characters. Each story should answer the following questions:

1. What was the problem that caused the character to procrastinate?
2. How was the problem solved?
3. What was the end result?

Each student should design a book cover for his or her story.

Curriculum Integration

Ask the students to paint their interpretations of the most "wonderful" picture in the class.

Visuals

- Display pictures of paintings created by famous artists.

THE BROTHERS WRONG AND WRONG AGAIN

by Louis Phillips

Synopsis

Join in the hilarious adventures of two backward brothers who do the most ordinary things in truly extraordinary manners. These brothers provide an amusing and entertaining tale.

Vocabulary

1. bureau
2. destruction
3. devouring
4. disbelief
5. ferocious
6. mend
7. occurred
8. pillaging
9. plundering
10. retreat
11. revived
12. surrender
13. suspended
14. trousers

Writing Activity

Ask each student to imagine that he or she is a member of a 20th century "Wrong" family. Have the students write descriptions of a typical backward day. (How would they dress, get to school, do their work, and play with their friends? What daily activities would they do with their families and how? What problems would be created by being backward?)

Each student should illustrate one aspect of his or her backward day.

Curriculum Integration

Allow the students to eat their lunches backward — dessert first! Let the students sign their names backward on all of their papers and write a backward note to a friend (for one day only!).

Visuals

• Enlarge pictures of Wrong and Wrong Again to show on the overhead projector.

DON'T FORGET THE BACON

by Pat Hutchins

Synopsis
Although repeating things over and over again usually helps a person to remember, this is not always the case as this story illustrates.

Vocabulary
1. clothes pegs

Writing Activity
Have each student create and illustrate a list of four items that could be purchased on a shopping trip. At an appointed time, each student may share his or her list and illustrations with a partner. Collect the illustrated lists. Proceed with another lesson for ten to fifteen minutes and then ask the students to list the items that they remember from their partners' lists.

Curriculum Integration
Play the "I went camping" game. Each student adds something he or she would take camping after repeating in order what the students before him or her chose. (It is easier to do when following an ABC pattern.)

Example:
I went camping and took an apple.
I went camping and took an apple and a bandage.

Visuals
- Gather pictures of six farm eggs, a cake for tea, a pound of pears, and bacon.

KING WACKY

by Dick Gackenbach

Synopsis

King Wacky is a most unusual king. Everything that Wacky does is backward — including his language. The royal wedding almost becomes a war due to the humorous occurrences!

Vocabulary

1. agreed	6. complained	11. prince
2. answer	7. fond	12. replaced
3. arrival	8. messenger	13. request
4. backward	9. permission	14. sprouts
5. commanded	10. popular	15. wacky

Writing Activity

Surprise the students by asking them to wear their clothing backward for an officially wacky day. Following the reading of Dick Gackenbach's *King Wacky,* declare each child a king or queen for the day. Give each student some official royal stationery on which to write a story about the day when he or she was king or queen of a country. Students may write serious or humorous stories to share with the group.

Curriculum Integration

Let the students use construction paper and glitter to make royal crowns!

Students may create royal castles using sugar cubes and construction paper and may design maps of royal countries on large sheets of paper.

Visuals

• Display pictures of royalty.

MISTER GAFFE

from **The Queen of Eene** *by Jack Prelutsky*

Synopsis
This is another of Jack Prelutsky's delightful character sketches concerning a peculiar gentleman who speaks in reverse.

Vocabulary
1. attempts
2. conversation
3. diner
4. discreetly
5. particular
6. peculiar
7. reversed

Writing Activity
Ask each student to create an imaginary character in his or her mind. Then ask the student to think of three questions that a reporter might ask someone in order to find out more about that person. After they have written their questions, have the students write the characters' responses as if they answered in reverse.

Curriculum Integration
Encourage the students to find out about differences in dialogue among English-speaking people around the world.

Visuals
- Allow the students to sample toast and cheese as they create their backward dialogues.

MRS. MINETTA'S CAR POOL

by Elizabeth Spurr

Synopsis
Riding in a car pool can be an out-of-the-ordinary experience as this story illustrates. Mrs. Minetta magically takes the children to the beach, to snowy hills, to an amusement park, and to a dude ranch where they enjoy glorious adventures.

Vocabulary

1.	absence	6.	habit	11.	tilted
2.	chauffeur	7.	promised	12.	toboggans
3.	convertible	8.	skimming	13.	traffic
4.	forbidden	9.	taught		

Writing Activity
Ask each student to decide which of the four locations where Mrs. Minetta took the children is his or her personal favorite. Chart the information for the class to see the results.

Illustrate mini "Mrs. Minetta's car pool" booklets. Motivate the students to write by allowing them to complete this sentence: The day Mrs. Minetta picked me up for school . . . .

Curriculum Integration
Paint murals in four sections. Assign a group of students to each section.

Dude Ranch Scenes
Winter Fun Scenes
Amusement Park Scenes
Beach Scenes

These four scenes also can provide topics for research. After conducting research, the students can fill their murals with as many accurate details as possible.

Visuals
- Display a beach towel, a shovel, boots, a sled, and some sand on a table.

MRS. PELOKI'S SNAKE

by Joanne Oppenheim

Synopsis

Bedlam occurs when Mrs. Peloki and her classroom think they have discovered a snake in the bathroom. Young readers will experience fear and laughter as they follow Mrs. Peloki's problem-solving adventure.

Vocabulary

1. emergency	6. scream
2. fake	7. slithering
3. hibernate	8. snake
4. measure	9. thinking
5. mistake	10. tongue

Writing Activity

This book is a wonderful lead-in to exploring a situation that seems to be scary but isn't really what it seems to be. Young authors may be able to recall a time when they thought something was not what it really was. Have the students write suspenseful stories that have unusual endings.

Curriculum Integration

Most families have a pet dog or cat, or perhaps an aquarium of fish. However, few families would choose a snake for a pet. Ask the students to question their parents about why they chose the pet(s) they did and why they might not have chosen a snake for a pet. Compile a chart or graph showing the information gathered by the class.

Visuals

- Display snake books and pictures.
- Discuss the students' feelings about snakes before reading the story.

MY MOM HATES ME IN JANUARY

by Judy Delton

Synopsis
Lee Henry's mother truly has the winter blues. She just can't seem to find enough activity to keep Lee Henry and herself at peace during the long winter. When the first signs of spring arrive, the tone of the book changes in an amusing way.

Vocabulary
1. radiator

Writing Activity
Lee Henry tells of Mom's "winter blues" behavior. Just as winter may make us blue, spring sometimes gives us a "fever." Ask the students to Brainstorm all of the good things that they think of when they hear the word spring. Write the following incomplete sentence on the board:

My mom loves me in the spring when

_____ .

Each student should choose his or her favorite idea to illustrate.

Curriculum Integration
Create two charts such as the ones below and have the students write their responses on the charts.

January		May	
Things I Like:	Things I don't like:	Things I like:	Things I don't like:

Visuals
- Display a collection of items that make you think of January.

THE SHERIFF OF ROTTENSHOT

by Jack Prelutsky

Synopsis
Spontaneous laughter will occur as the young reader enjoys the twists and turns of the language in Jack Prelutsky's poetry.

Vocabulary

1. bristles
2. britches
3. gadget
4. habitat
5. million
6. monstrous
7. rodent
8. saddle
9. sheriff
10. soggy
11. spaghetti
12. squirmed
13. tinkering
14. tough
15. transforms

Writing Activity
Instruct the students to list rhyming words found in Jack Prelutsky's poems. Ask the students to use the rhyming words to create poems about the world.

Curriculum Integration
Let each student make a tinfoil sheriff's badge after reading the poem *The Sheriff of Rottenshot* (patterns on next page).

Have the students use spaghetti noodles, food coloring and glue to make designs on wax paper after reading the poem *The Spaghetti Nut*.

Visuals
- additional books by Jack Prelutsky

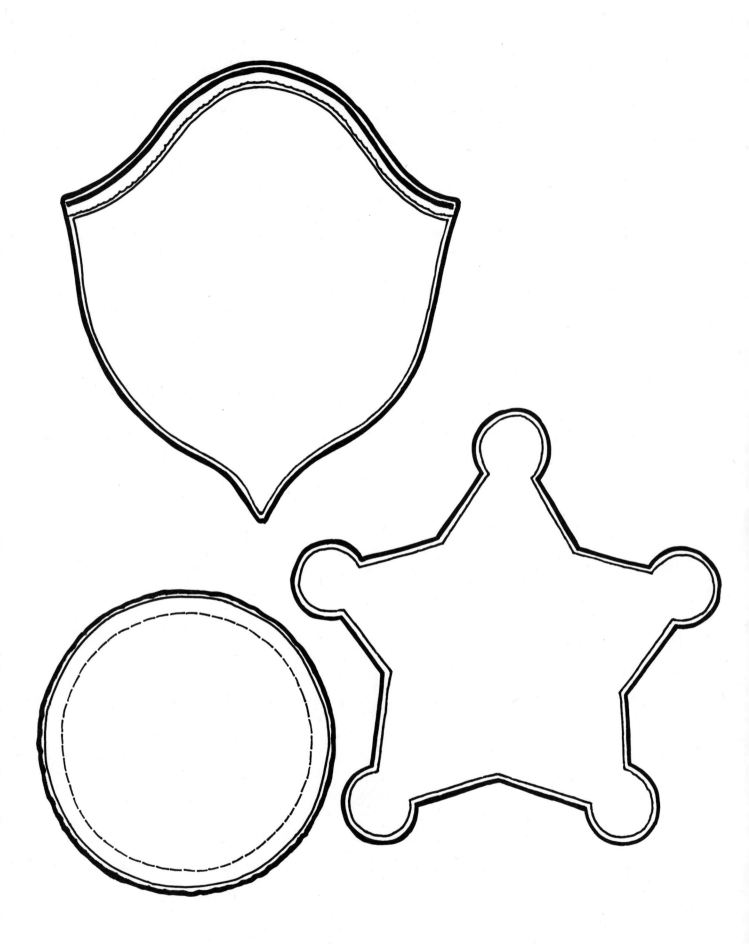

RALPH'S SECRET WEAPON

by Steven Kellogg

Synopsis
Ralph stays with Aunt Georgiana for the summer and finds out that she has some pretty ambitious plans for him. When Ralph is declared a hopeless bassoon player, his aunt decides that he should get rid of the giant sea serpent that is terrorizing the U.S. Navy. The results are hilarious.

Vocabulary
1. admiral
2. bassoon
3. Colosseum (Coliseum)
4. contestants
5. dismissed
6. exhausted
7. frantic
8. immediately
9. instantly
10. international
11. nibbling
12. shrieked
13. slithering
14. successfully
15. talented
16. thunderous

Writing Activity
Allow the students to cut out and color sea serpent masks. Then have each student write what the sea serpent might have said to describe how the "secret weapon" affected him. Have students wear their masks and tell their stories.

Curriculum Integration
Have the students research to find facts about the bassoon. Locate samples of bassoon music and compare the bassoon to other musical instruments.

Visuals
- Steven Kellogg's illustrations
- a picture of a bassoon
- snake pictures

Serpent Mask

THERE'S NOTHING TO DO!

by James Stevenson

Synopsis
Mary Ann and Louie complain to their grandpa about how bored they are. Grandpa triggers their imaginations with hilarious stories of his boyhood.

Vocabulary

1. burrow	5. exactly	8. moment	11. twisted
2. consideration	6. grabbed	9. slim	12. whirled
3. disappeared	7. grip	10. trail	13. yawning
4. dozing			

Writing Activity
Have the students write and illustrate mini-cartoon booklets (one sentence per page and an action word in each picture).

Curriculum Integration
Create a cartoon corner to spark students' imaginations:

1. Display Ed Emberly's books.
2. Display newspaper comic sections.
3. Display old comic books.

Visuals
- Create a display of childrens' drawing books.

TODAY WAS A TERRIBLE DAY

by Patricia Reilly Giff

Synopsis
Ronald's day at school begins badly and ends much worse. His teacher thinks of a way to help him feel better about himself.

Vocabulary
1. mariners
2. monitor
3. noticed
4. satellite
5. terrible

Writing Activity
Ask the students to close their eyes and to visualize Ronald Morgan arriving at their homes after his terrible day at school. He has lost the note from his teacher. Tell the students that it is their responsibility to make Ronald feel better about himself. What would they say or do? Have the students write and illustrate new story endings.

Curriculum Integration
Ronald was given the nickname "Snakey." Students should poll their classmates to find out how many of them have nicknames and how many of those students like their nicknames. Help the students find a way to graph this information. Discuss the importance of charts and graphs and how they can enhance research.

Visuals
* Share with the students any experiences you have had with a nickname.

WHAT'S UNDER MY BED?

by James Stevenson

Synopsis
Once again Grandpa comes to the rescue as Mary Ann and Louie are scared of what might be under their beds. After Grandpa explains what was under his bed when he was their age, all are set for a good night's sleep.

Vocabulary
1. creaking
2. especially
3. glittery
4. stilts
5. wailing

Writing Activity
Grandpa's window allowed a wide variety of imaginary creatures to come into his room — "creatures that reached and pinched and poked, nibbled and dribbled, snapped and stomped and squished." Have each student create an imaginary group of "boogie monsters" who won't allow children to sleep at night and make a list of eight to ten action words describing the scary creatures' behaviors.

Curriculum Integration
Create "monster cookies" as a treat to scare away those imaginary creatures from under the bed!

Monster Cookies

12 eggs	1 lb. butter
2 lbs. brown sugar	3 lbs. peanut butter
4 lbs. white sugar	18 cups quick oatmeal
1 tbs. syrup	1 lb. M&M's
5 tsp. soda	1 lb. chocolate chips

Mix ingredients in order listed above. Flatten well. Bake at 350 degrees for 12 minutes. Do not overbake!

Visuals
- Create a darkened room in which there are strange noises and an occasional ghost or bat.

DEMI'S FIND THE ANIMAL ABC

by Demi

Synopsis
Exercise your observational skills by locating all of the animals hidden in the beautiful illustrations of this ABC book.

Vocabulary
1. armadillo
2. ibis
3. jaguar
4. observation
5. vole
6. yak

Writing Activity
Have the students compile individual ABC lists of animals not mentioned in the book. (They may need to use several types of reference books to make their lists as complete as possible.)

> Examples:
> A = aardvark
> B = badger
> C = cougar
> D = donkey
> E = eagle

Then let each student compile a book of factual information about his or her favorite five animals. Students should hunt for obscure, interesting facts about each of the animals they choose. Instruct the students to sketch the animal for each entry.

Curriculum Integration
Let the students try animal calligraphy. In this artistic endeavor, the name of the animal becomes the animal itself (see the example on this page).

Visual
- The book is the visual and must be used with small groups.

JUMANJI

by Chris Van Allsburg

Synopsis
Two children discover a board game in which the animals and sounds come to life. Students will respond to a feeling of danger and adventure experienced by the two children.

Vocabulary

1. adventure	4. disappointed	7. reaches	10. silence
2. boring	5. firmly	8. scarf	11. stampede
3. breath	6. jungle	9. scrambled	12. upset

Writing Activity
Let each student create his or her very own game. Provide tagboard, dice, spinners, and other supplies for the students to use. Emphasize the importance of writing clear directions.

Curriculum Integration
Let each student bring a game from home to share with the class.

Instruct each student to research a wild animal and report to the group something new that he or she learned.

Students also may research volcanoes. Let the students look through science textbooks and resource books to discover how to make a volcano model.

Visuals
* books about wild animals and volcanoes

TAKE ANOTHER LOOK

by Tana Hoban

Synopsis
The pictures in this photographic glance at the world will spark the imaginations of students.

Vocabulary
This is a wordless picture book. Ask the students to help create a list of vocabulary words to describe the photographs.

Writing Activity
Instruct each student to choose one photograph and to write what he or she sees at first glance and then what details he or she notices upon looking more closely.

You may wish to prepare "peek-a-boo" picture cards to use as story starters. Conceal an interesting picture except for one small window through which the student may look (half of a file folder "sealed" with four fasteners; picture glued inside; hole cut out to make a window). While looking through the window, the student should write a story that he or she believes will fit the setting that is partially exposed. After sharing the story with the class, the student may open the window.

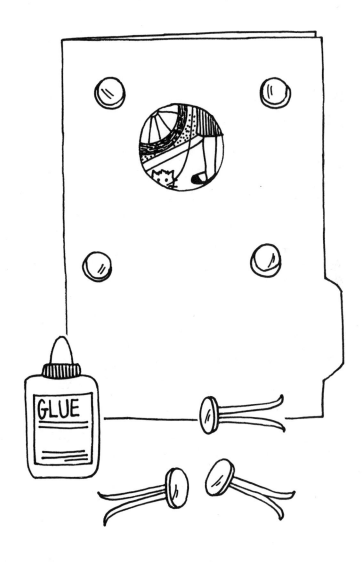

Curriculum Integration
Allow each student to take one photograph during a photograph excursion. After the pictures have been developed, have each young photographer cover his or her print with a piece of construction paper, exposing a circle of the print. Discuss the reactions to these individually-made "take another look" photos.

Research optical illusions and photography.

Visuals
• Display camera books, optical illusion books, and photography books.

UNRIDDLING

by Alvin Schwartz

Synopsis
Alvin Schwartz presents the reader with eighteen different types of riddles. Although the book is recommended for ages nine and up, it is great "thinking" material for younger academically talented children.

Vocabulary
The vocabulary will vary with the type of riddle being explored.

Writing Activity
Have the students devise their own rebus riddles (as presented on pages 43 plus in *Unriddling*). Students should write their solutions on the backs of their papers.

Students may create original "Droodles" (as presented on pages 20 plus in *Unriddling*). The students should write explanations on the backs of their droodles.

Curriculum Integration
Each student can conduct a search for a riddle that he or she thinks will stump classmates. Assemble a class book of "stumpers" with a page of solutions in the back of the book.

Visuals
- Create and display a large rebus as an example of how to solve a rebus.

WHERE'S WALDO?

by Martin Handford

Synopsis
Waldo the hiker is cleverly concealed amidst intriguingly detailed travel pictures. The reader is to uncover his secret whereabouts along the travel route. Additional missing items require location along the way.

Vocabulary

1. amazing	5. capsized	9. knight	13. snorkel
2. armor	6. Egyptian	10. mallet	14. spectacles
3. binoculars	7. incredible	11. mummy	15. trousers
4. canal	8. javelins	12. smuggler	

Writing Activity
Ask the students to pretend that they have visited one of the places found along Waldo's hike. Have each student develop a list of adjectives and phrases that describe the scene. Next, allow the students to choose one of the other characters found in the setting and to write a brief paragraph about what the character was doing at that particular place. Students should try to make the characters as believable as possible through the use of description.

Curriculum Integration
Instruct each student to locate a detail in an illustration that he or she knows could not possibly exist as presented in the story. Each student should write a convincing rationale explaining why the detail does not make sense and how it could be changed to better fit its setting. (Remind the students that the incongruous details are added for humor.)

Visuals
- Share the book's pictures in small groups.

THE WRECK OF THE ZEPHYR

by Chris Van Allsburg

Synopsis

The wreck of a small abandoned sailboat intrigues the reader as the story opens. An old man tells the tale of a young boy's adventure on the boat.

Vocabulary

1. blustery	4. ominous	7. sailor	10. village
2. harbor	5. oyster stew	8. search	11. whistled
3. hoisted	6. reef	9. strange	

Writing Activity

Ask the students to imagine that they are sailors and that their boats can travel by sea or air. Have the students write and illustrate stories about their adventures. Students should use descriptive words to tell about the things they see from their boats.

Curriculum Integration

Have a class boat-making contest. Students must use drawing paper and transparent tape to make their boats. Each boat must be no more than four inches wide and six inches long. The boat is to be placed in a long trough containing two inches of water to see how many seconds it takes for the boat to sail to the end of the trough. Supply power with a small fan. Let the students make a number of boats and graph the results.

Visuals

- world map
- books about boats
- small fan
- long trough

A SWEETHEART FOR VALENTINE

by Lorna Balian

Synopsis
A baby arrives unexpectedly in a basket at the village of St. Valentine. The unusual little girl in the basket continues to grow until she becomes a "giant" of a young lady. Everyone in the village becomes involved in trying to find a perfect mate for Valentine.

Vocabulary
1. absolutely
2. disposition
3. disturbance
4. lowing
5. roused
6. scurrying

Writing Activity
Let the students write their own stories about how Valentine's Day has come to be. Students also might enjoy creating imaginary diaries of "a week in the life of Valentine" for the week before Valentine's wedding.

Curriculum Integration
Ask the students to create a special wedding dress for Valentine. Have the students list the materials that would be needed to construct the dress. Let each student draw a colorful picture of his or her special creation.

Visuals
- the illustrations from the book
- books about giants

A VALENTINE FOR COUSIN ARCHIE

by Barbara Williams

Synopsis
An unsigned valentine causes excitement as each animal dreams about his secret admirer. The reactions of the animals to their personal valentines produce an amusing story.

Vocabulary
1. bellowing
2. crab grass
3. dainty
4. doilies
5. lumbago
6. opossum
7. repellent
8. thermos
9. widow

Writing Activity
Have the students draw names so that each child has a "secret valentine pal." Instruct each student to make a valentine and to write a valentine message which gives hints about the chosen person's identity. (The students should sign their names.) Display the valentines around the room and let the students try to find their valentines. After a few minutes, instruct everyone to return to their seats as you distribute the valentines to their rightful owners. Students will enjoy finding out if their guesses were correct.

Example:
Dear Valentine,
    You are a pretty blond.
    You play baseball well.
    I like the yellow shirt
        you're wearing today.
        Your Secret Valentine Pal,
            Joe

Curriculum Integration
Create an animal chart that distinguishes the real animals from the make-believe animals in the story (see next page).

Animal	Real	Make-Believe
1. chipmunk	✓	
2. rabbit	✓	
3. opossum	✓	

Visuals
- Use the torn valentine list from the story and the pattern below to make a visual.

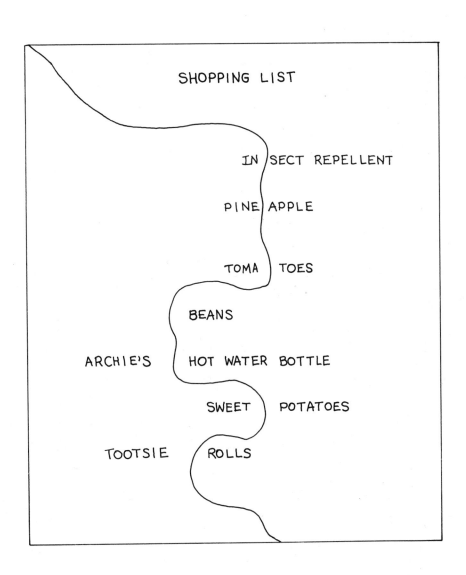

SHOPPING LIST

IN SECT REPELLENT

PINE APPLE

TOMA TOES

BEANS

ARCHIE'S HOT WATER BOTTLE

SWEET POTATOES

TOOTSIE ROLLS

BEE MY VALENTINE

by Miriam Cohen

Synopsis
Young children will delight in the shared experiences of giving valentines on Valentine's Day.

Vocabulary
1. harmonica
2. kazoo
3. xylophone

Writing Activity
A pun is created by using a word in a new or humorous way to suggest a different meaning. Puns used for valentines in the book include:
1. My two-lips are thine
2. Police be my valentine
3. Bee my honey

Students will enjoy creating original puns to write on individually-designed valentines.

Curriculum Integration
Brainstorm a list of bugs — spiders, ants, etc. Instruct the students to create bug puns and to gather factual information about each bug.

Example: I "spider" sitting next to him.

Facts:
A spider is not a true insect. It is an arachnid. A spider has three main body parts.

Visuals
- Give a valentine that has a pun written on it to each student.

THE BEST VALENTINE IN THE WORLD

by Marjorie Sharmat

Synopsis
Ferdinand Fox wants to create the best valentine in the world for his friend Florette. When Valentine's Day arrives, a strange turn of events occurs.

Vocabulary
1. celebrating
2. descriptions
3. deserves
4. masterpiece
5. permanent
6. standards

Writing Activity
Read pages 7 to 15 ("Ferdinand telephoned Florette. 'What have you been doing lately?' said Ferdinand.") Students can create a beginning and an ending for the story. Then read the story in its entirety to the group.

Curriculum Integration
Students can create valentines of unusual colors for friends (such as the ones given by Ferdinand and Florette in the story). Students may use any colors except pink and red.

Instruct the students to research the origin of the valentine.

Visuals
- Introduce the story by giving each student a valentine.

Freckles And Willie

by Margery Cuyler

Synopsis
Willie learns much about friendship and caring with the help of his faithful dog, Freckles.

Vocabulary
1. allergic
2. aluminum foil
3. barely
4. construction paper
5. desert
6. whimpered

Writing Activity
Have the students create "prose party poppers." Each student will need a bathroom tissue paper tube, a piece of tissue paper (approximately eight inches longer than the tube), and two pieces of yarn or ribbon. Give each student a copy of the following student page and instruct the students to create endings to the introductory statements. The students should fold their heart-shaped messages and place them in the tubes. (You may wish to add a piece of candy, a balloon, etc.) Then the students should wrap the tubes in tissue paper and tie the end with yarn or ribbon. Place the "prose party poppers" in a bag and let each student grab one to read and enjoy!

Curriculum Integration
Students may want to create special valentines for their pets.

Visuals
• the book's illustrations

My Friend

A friend is special to me because _____

I can always count on a friend to _____

I am a good friend because _____

Signed, _____

"A friend is a present which you give yourself."

Robert Louis Stevenson

THE GREAT VALENTINE'S DAY BALLOON RACE

by Adrienne Adams

Synopsis
The rabbit family celebrates Valentine's Day in an unusual manner. Bonnie has a grand idea to build a hot-air balloon and race it on Valentine's Day. The plans for the important event are a success and Bonnie becomes a heroine.

Vocabulary
1. decorated
2. goose pimples
3. gorgeous
4. imagine
5. impatience

Writing Activity
Ask the students to create new endings for the story. Ask these questions: If Orson and Bonnie did not win the race, could it still be a "Valentine" story? What would happen to Orson and Bonnie's balloon?

Curriculum Integration
Students may create their own hot-air balloons by using crepe paper for the tops and paper cups for the baskets.

Perform the following experiment:

You will need a balloon, a bottle, very hot water (122+ degrees) and a bowl. Put the balloon over the bottle's opening and set the bottle in the bowl of hot water. As the water heats the air in the bottle, the balloon will inflate. Air is a gas. As the air is heated, it expands and inflates the balloon.

Visuals
- Create a large, multi-colored hot-air balloon.

THE MYSTERIOUS VALENTINE

by Nancy Carlson

Synopsis
On Valentine's Day, someone sends Louanne a valentine signed, "From your secret admirer." Find out with Louanne who that admirer might be.

Vocabulary
1. determined
2. mentioned
3. peered

Writing Activity
Have each student prepare a large construction paper valentine and write three clues about his or her identity on the valentine. Exchange the valentines with the students in another class who, in turn, will try to guess the identities of their secret admirers. (The students may choose to write their clues in riddle form.)

In addition, each student may choose a famous person (living or deceased) to whom he or she would like to send a secret-admirer valentine. Ask the students to write short stories about how they would deliver their valentines to their chosen celebrities.

Curriculum Integration
People often send chocolate on Valentine's Day. Have the students brainstorm a list of animals and a list of what these animals might give to their sweethearts for Valentine's Day.

Visuals
• Give mysterious secret-admirer valentines to the students.

SOME THINGS GO TOGETHER

by Charlotte Zolotow

Synopsis
This is a beautiful collection of simple verse celebrating those things that just seem to "go together."

Vocabulary
1. dove
2. moth
3. pigeons
4. prance

Writing Activity
Encourage the students to create short rhymes of things that go together. The students may illustrate their rhymes.

Example:

_____ with _____
_____ with _____

Curriculum Integration
Students may create special valentines with short rhyming verses to give to special friends.

Visuals
- A treat that "goes together" would be fun to share.

  Suggestions:
  milk and cookies
  root beer and ice cream

THE VALENTINE BEARS

by Eve Bunting

Synopsis
Mrs. Bear is determined to celebrate the Valentine's Day holiday. She awakens Mr. Bear from hibernation with favorite treats and loving poems. Mr. Bear surprises his valentine with delightful chocolate-covered ants.

Vocabulary
1. admired
2. decided
3. huddled
4. muzzle
5. secure
6. sleeked

Writing Activity
Let the students make special valentines (see pattern below) on which to write original valentine poems about special persons.

Put picture inside heart.

Write poem here.

Punch holes around edge and thread yarn through holes.

Curriculum Integration
Have the students research to find out how Valentine's Day is celebrated in other countries.

Let each student create a valentine treat box for someone he or she loves. Instruct the student to write a special message to his or her "special someone" and to put the message inside the box.

Visuals
- Decorate a small box with hearts and put valentine treats inside the box to share with the students.

WAKE UP, GROUNDHOG

by Carol Cohen

Synopsis
We assume that the groundhog will automatically come out of his home to let us know if winter will continue or if spring is on its way. But what would happen if the groundhog didn't want to get up? This amusing book answers that question.

Vocabulary
1. appointment
2. delivered
3. hourglass
4. oblige
5. slyly

Writing Activity
Stop reading midway through the story. Ask the students to devise a foolproof plan for waking up the goundhog.

Discuss what other animals would be good "barometers" for spring if the goundhog did not already hold this position. Ask each student to choose an animal and to write a story about how this animal became the official indicator of spring.

Curriculum Integration
Learn more about groundhogs as a class. How did the groundhog's shadow become a forecaster of spring?

Visuals
- Use a large picture of a groundhog as the catalyst for a preliminary discussion.

BIG MOSE: HERO FIREMAN

by Harold W. Felton

Synopsis
Tall tale character Big Mose develops an unusual method for putting out a fire when the roof flies off of a burning building.

Vocabulary
1.	brass	6.	grimly
2.	cobblestone	7.	protect
3.	demanded	8.	steeples
4.	enthusiastically	9.	volunteer
5.	exclaimed	10.	wobbles

Writing Activity
Each student should try to formulate an important fire-prevention tip. Ask each one to write and illustrate his or her tip on poster board. Then have the students share their tips with the class.

Curriculum Integration
In an effort to learn more about modern-day firefighting techniques, invite a member of the local fire department to visit the class and show equipment and discuss procedures. Have the students formulate questions before the visit. (Do we still have volunteer fire-fighters today? How long does it take on average to respond to a fire? How are firefighters notified of a fire? etc.)

Visuals
- Wear a fire hat and/or display firefighting equipment.
- Display pictures of fires and discuss the seriousness of fires.

GRANDPA'S FARM

by James Flora

Synopsis
Grandpa loves to engage in the art of exaggeration. In fact, he is an expert at it. Join in the fun of listening to grandpa's stories of long ago.

Note: This book may take two or more sittings to read.

Vocabulary
1. gravity
2. hitched
3. slave
4. shivering
5. smokestack
6. steamboat
7. thawed

Writing Activity
Grandpa didn't have enough pages to tell the story about the "big snow of '44." Allow the students to work in pairs to write this story. Review some of the more prominent exaggerations in the book, and remind the students to include much exaggeration in their stories.

Curriculum Integration
Let each student paint a colorful picture of one of the delightful exaggerations from the book.

For example:
1. The wind was so strong that it blew my eyebrows down to my chin.
2. It (the cornstalk) was growing so fast that I could never chop it twice in the same place.
3. It was so cold that our shadows froze on the ground.
4. At that very moment gravity froze.
5. A new cow started to grow on that old tail.

Visuals
- Display pictures of farms and farm life.

THE GREAT BIG ESPECIALLY BEAUTIFUL EASTER EGG

by James Stevenson

Synopsis

Grandpa tells about his dangerous and difficult trip to find the world's most enormous Easter egg. The facetious illustrations of Grandpa on his travels will produce moments of laughter.

Vocabulary

1. blizzard
2. foggiest
3. obviously
4. recall
5. violets

Writing Activity

As the students become more comfortable with writing, they will gradually pay more attention to the details involved in creating a good story. Each story needs to have a distinct beginning, middle, and ending. The beginning should entice the reader to read on and should help the reader become familiar with the setting and the characters. The middle should present a problem or other action. The ending should resolve the problem or conclude the action. Ask the students to identify the beginning, middle, and ending of the story you have just read. Ask the students to write one or two sentences about each section and to illustrate the sections.

James Stevenson uses a cartoon approach in portions of his book. Have the students create a brief tall tale cartoon for a portion of another tall tale.

Curriculum Integration

Send the students on an investigative search for the smallest and the largest eggs in the world. The students may use any reference books available to them.

Visuals

● the book's illustrations

JOHN HENRY AND PAUL BUNYAN PLAY BASEBALL

by Wyatt Blassingame

Synopsis
When John Henry and Paul Bunyan fail to make a baseball team because of their tremendous strength, a match-up of the two superheroes is finally arranged. The results constitute a "happily ever after" ending for fans of both heroes.

Vocabulary
1. ashore
2. cotton bales
3. downpour
4. gangplank
5. lumberjack
6. manager
7. rookie
8. spike
9. timber
10. tremendous

Writing Activity
Instruct each student to develop a new tall tale hero or heroine on the *"My Tall Tale Hero/Heroine"* student page. Discuss the importance of character development in a story and ways that the author can make his or her character "come alive" for the reader.

After each young author has fully described and developed a character, ask the students to illustrate their characters.

Curriculum Integration
Children need to become tellers of tales. Ask each student to find out about other Paul Bunyan adventures and to share an adventure with the class or a small group.

Visuals
- Create larger-than-life pictures of John Henry and Paul Bunyan to display in the classroom.

Name _____

MY TALL TALE HERO/HEROINE

Develop a new tall tale hero or heroine.
Describe the character in the space below.
Then illustrate the character.

_____
(Character's name)

_____

_____

_____

_____

_____

_____

_____

_____

McBROOM AND THE BIG WIND

by Sid Fleishman

Synopsis
Josh McBroom is indeed a teller of tall tales. Readers will delight in the exaggerations of the big wind.

Vocabulary
1. barge	7. deny	13. prairie	18. to and fro
2. barrel staves	8. haystacks	14. raged	19. topsoil
3. battered	9. heaved	15. rambunctious	20. trifling
4. brace	10. ornery	16. splendid	21. zephyr
5. buttercups	11. planks	17. tangling	

Writing Activity
Ask the students to complete the *"Tall Tale Thrillers"* student page.

Curriculum Integration
Have the students investigate big winds that are threatening to property and people. Ask the students to classify these winds into categories such as hurricanes, tornadoes, etc. Then challenge the students to find examples in history of each kind of wind. Students can take turns reporting the destruction caused by each "wind disaster."

Visuals
- books of tall tales

Name _____

TALL TALE THRILLERS

Complete the sentences below.

1. It was so windy that _____

   _____ .

2. The biscuits were so heavy that we could use them to _____

   _____ .

3. The draft was so strong that it _____

   _____ .

4. Josh McBroom told such *tall* tales that _____

   _____ .

5. After the big wind, it was so quiet that _____

   _____ .

   Illustrate one "thriller" below:

MRS. GADDY AND THE FAST-GROWING VINE

by Wilson Gage

Synopsis
When Mrs. Gaddy's vine threatens to overtake her happy home, she must resort to drastic measures.

Vocabulary
1. molasses
2. pruning shears
3. shoots
4. snapdragons
5. storm cellar
6. vine

Writing Activity
Stop reading the story when you reach page 21. (Mrs. Gaddy is about to hitch her wagon and drive to town.) Have each student write a cure for stopping the fast-growing vine. Share the cures orally. Then read the end of the story.

Curriculum Integration
Plant some fast-growing plants (peas, beans, etc.) and some slow-growing plants (squash). Have the students observe and chart the differences in the plants' development. Ask the students to find information about the kinds of plants that are considered to be vining plants. Chart the differences between vining and non-vining plants.

Visuals
- Bring vining plants or snapdragons to class for the students to observe.

PECOS BILL CATCHES
A HIDEBEHIND

by Wyatt Blassingame

Synopsis
The ever-popular Pecos Bill faces a new, exciting challenge as he tries to catch the elusive hidebehind. Join the fun as exaggeration after exaggeration stretches the imagination and leads to a comical adventure.

Vocabulary
1. buck
2. corral
3. embarrassment
4. lasso
5. quail
6. stirrups

Writing Activity
Review some of the tall tale characters and their unusual capabilities (the goofus bird, tea kettlers, and roperites). Ask each student to create a new tall tale character and to write about the special things that the character can do. Have the students illustrate their tall tale characters.

Curriculum Integration
Discuss cacti. Let the class observe a cactus if one is available. Ask the students to read about the areas where cacti grow to find out what other types of plants might grow there as well.

Visuals
• a cactus

WHOPPERS: TALL TALES AND OTHER LIES

by Alvin Schwartz

Synopsis
This is a wonderful collection of delightful whoppers. The humorous introduction about "Hard Lying" really lends itself to the development of tall tale telling.

Vocabulary
Vocabulary will vary with the stories chosen. Skim the selection for appropriate words to discuss. (Be sure to read the introduction on "Hard Lying.")

Writing Activity
The "ordinary people shoppers" will give some insight into tall tale character development. Give each student a *"Tall Tale Development Guide"* to use in developing a tall tale.

Curriculum Integration
Have each student create a "whopper puzzle" by cutting a picture of a tall tale into puzzle pieces. Students may exchange puzzles and try to guess what tall tales the puzzles represent.

Visuals
- Create a picture of a tall tale or "whopper" to share with the class.

Name _____

TALL TALE DEVELOPMENT GUIDE

Follow these steps to write a tall tale about a tall character!

1. Think about the tall tale character you want to create. Choose either the girl or boy pattern to use in building your character. Color the character's face with crayons or markers.
2. Write the tall tale on the story sheets provided.
3. Tape the story sheets to the character's face as shown below to create a very tall character!

Write notes below to plan your story:

Once upon a time there lived _____

_____

_____

_____

_____

_____

_____

_____

_____

_____

_____

_____

_____ had many adventures.

On one adventure _____

_____

_____

_____

_____

_____

_____

_____

_____

_____

_____

Then one day _____

_____

_____

_____

_____

_____

_____

_____

_____

_____

_____

_____

THE END

SPRING

THE COUNTRY BUNNY AND THE LITTLE GOLD SHOES

by DuBose Heyward

Synopsis

The five kindest, swiftest, and wisest bunnies are always chosen by Grandfather Bunny to be the "Easter Bunnies" of the world. This heartwarming story tells how one extraordinary bunny takes her place among the five.

Vocabulary

1. budding
2. clever
3. land
4. laurel
5. linen
6. precious
7. select
8. swiftest
9. whisked

Writing Activity

The Country Bunny has several problems to overcome in the story. Have the students compile a list of the bunny's problems. Then discuss how each problem was solved. Ask each student to write about a problem that he or she has had and how he or she solved it (or could have solved it better). Help the students understand that creative problem solving can apply to even the smallest daily problem.

Curriculum Integration

Allow each student to paint a picture of his or her idea of the most beautiful egg in the world.

Visuals

- stuffed bunnies
- Flack's illustrations

The Easter Pig

By Louise McClenathan

Synopsis

Pig grows restless during the pre-Easter season and longs to "carve out" a holiday nitch for herself. She wants to have a "pig holiday" in much the same way that rabbits and groundhogs have special occasions. She sets out to accomplish this in an unusual way.

Vocabulary

1. bounded	8. occurred	15. roused	22. strutted
2. dreary	9. paced	16. rumbled	23. swooped
3. flexed	10. peered	17. scuttled	24. treasure
4. fond	11. perched	18. slats	25. trinket
5. fretfully	12. preening	19. smudged	26. trough
6. merrily	13. proper	20. splendor	27. venture out
7. murmured	14. roam	21. strangled	28. wicked

Writing Activity

Stop reading the story at the point where the Easter Rabbit and the Easter Pig meet. ("I'd like to work with you and be the Easter Pig. This is my first trip outside the pen.") Allow the students to write and illustrate their own story endings. After the students have shared their compositions, finish reading the story.

Curriculum Integration

Ask the young researchers to find out about the origin of the traditional Easter rabbit. Specifically, ask the students to find out how, where, when and why the tradition began, and how the tradition has changed over the years. Discuss ways in which the students celebrate Easter in their homes.

Visuals

- Display an Easter basket filled with traditional Easter goodies plus one "Easter Pig" novelty.

LEPRECHAUNS NEVER LIE

by Lorna Balian

Synopsis

Gram becomes ill and must rely on Ninny Nanny who is too lazy to care for either of them. Ninny Nanny decides to catch a leprechaun to end their troubles. The leprechaun seems to be unusually wise and helps them to solve their problems in a creative way.

Vocabulary

1. banshee
2. blathering
3. boasted
4. britches
5. dawdled
6. fetch
7. glen
8. mite
9. naught
10. nestled
11. raving
12. scowled
13. spade
14. thatch
15. vanished
16. witless

Writing Activity

Let the students become involved in forecasting. Each student should choose one of the characters from the story and write a paragraph predicting a future event that will occur in that character's life. As each student shares his or her predictions, classmates can guess who the character is. (Students can illustrate their forecasts if they have time.)

Curriculum Integration

Instruct the students to find answers for the following questions:

1. How many teachers in our school are Irish?
2. How many stories are there in the library about leprechauns?
3. Where is Ireland located on the map?
4. Who was St. Patrick? How many students in the class know about the legend of St. Patrick?
5. How many students in our room would choose green as their favorite color?
6. What is meant by the phrase, "The luck of the Irish"?

7. What "good luck" superstitions do members of our class have?

Visuals

- Display an assortment of pictures that have become symbols of St. Patrick's Day.

THE LEPRECHAUN'S STORY

by Richard Kennedy

Synopsis

When a tradesman walking down an Irish road spots a leprechaun, he is sure the leprechaun is bound to lead him to a pot of gold. However, if the tradesman looks away for even a moment, the leprechaun will disappear. Students will listen eagerly to find out who wins this war of wits.

Vocabulary

1. ascent	7. glanced	13. misfortune	17. steadily
2. charity	8. grubs	14. plight	18. strolling
3. cobblers	9. hedgerow	15. profit	19. tradesman
4. ease	10. journey	16. skiff	20. wits
5. feeble	11. lass		

Writing Activity

Stop reading after the sentence, "The devil himself has popped up behind ye!" Ask the students to think of another impending tragedy that they could describe if they were the leprechaun trying to trick the tradesman. Have the students illustrate their ideas. After the students have shared their ideas, finish reading the story.

Curriculum Integration

Let the students create their own leprechaun comic strip character. Then have the students create a character that the leprechaun could try to trick.

Visuals

- pictures of leprechauns
- pots of "gold"
- shamrocks

THE PINKISH, PURPLISH, BLUISH EGG

by Bill Peet

Synopsis

The peace-loving dove experiences the empty-nest syndrome when she discovers an untended egg. She patiently hatches the egg and finds an unusual half-animal, half-bird creature inside it. Although the neighbors distrust him, this new creature proves his worth by performing an unusual service.

Vocabulary

1. admire	9. fabulous	17. illegal	25. slugs
2. astounded	10. faint	18. instincts	26. stunned
3. bewildered	11. flocking	19. jeered	27. swooped
4. bleak	12. frantically	20. marvel	28. violence
5. brute	13. furious	21. mocked	29. woebegone
6. commotion	14. gigantic	22. precaution	
7. depressed	15. gleefully	23. scoundrel	
8. determined	16. grubworms	24. scowl	

Writing Activity

Read the story through page 9. At this point, ask the students to write a few sentences about what they think will be hatched from the egg. Then have the students draw the cracked egg and the creature that was hatched from it. Mount the illustrations on construction paper.

Curriculum Integration

Have the students create a dual animal. The top of the animal should be of one type and the bottom of another.

Example:
Biraffe — half bird, half giraffe

Visuals

• Bill Peet's illustrations

THE AMAZING PIG

by Paul Galdone

Synopsis
What could be more amazing than a pig who stands on his nose? What about a pig who stands on his nose and decides to leave the farm, seek his fortune, and join the circus! We see that the grass is not always greener on the other side of the fence as we travel with the Amazing Pig on his amazing journey.

Vocabulary
1. amazing
2. clever
3. declared
4. disappointed
5. inherited
6. journey
7. pantry
8. peasant
9. permitted
10. swineherd

Writing Activity
Have the students write (and illustrate) newspaper ads to sell their own amazing pigs. Discuss advertising and the things that will or will not sell a product.

Curriculum Integration
Let the students work in groups to find other stories about pigs. Then, have each group write a character sketch of the pig in their group's story. The character sketches should include:

The story title
A physical description of the pig
Personality characteristics of the pig
An adventure the pig had, or how the pig solved a problem
A contrast of the pig with the Amazing Pig

Visuals
- Display pictures of pigs.
- Tell the story through the use of a pig hand puppet.

BUBBA AND BABBA

by Maria Polushkin

Synopsis
Bubba and Babba are two very lazy bears who have an argument about doing the dishes. They finally solve their problem by making a humorous and unusual pact.

Vocabulary
1. chattering
2. porridge
3. puttering
4. repay
5. toil
6. unpleasant
7. wilt

Writing Activity
Instruct each student to write a cure for laziness.

Have each student write a plan for a fair way to divide the chores in his or her family or the family of Bubba and Babba.

Curriculum Integration
This folk tale originated in Russia. Have the students locate Russia on the map and then find three facts about the culture of Russia. (Has the Russian culture made the folk tale of Bubba and Babba any different from one that might originate in the United States?)

Visuals
• the book's illustrations

FABLES

by Arnold Lobel

Synopsis

Arnold Lobel presents a delightful array of fables for the young reader. A lesson is outlined at the end of each fable. Students will enjoy trying to figure out the lesson after a fable has been read.

Vocabulary

1. admired
2. alarmed
3. alluring
4. flattery
5. hollyhocks
6. observation
7. order
8. resist
9. seldom
10. terrors

Writing Activity

Give each student a copy of the *"Fable Fact Sheet"* and read the sheet aloud.

When Arnold Lobel was asked in an interview how he wrote his book *Fables*, he said that first he made a list of animals about which he would like to write. Let the class brainstorm for such a list. Then have each student choose an animal about which to write an original fable. Remind the students to tell a moral or teach a lesson in their stories. Compile the fables to make a class book.

Curriculum Integration

As a science activity, have each student choose an animal to research. Discuss the qualities of each animal. (How does Lobel use "artistic liberty" in creating his fables?)

Visuals

- Share animal picture cards with the class before reading the story. Ask the students to discuss how each animal might bring a story to mind.

FABLE FACT SHEET

In 1981 Arnold Lobel, well-known for his books about Frog and Toad, received the Caldecott Medal for his book *Fables*. His books, written in an old literary form, make fables new and exciting for children of all ages.

However, fables are far from being new. In fact, it has been speculated that fables originated around 800 B.C. Fables originally were not intended to be stories for children. Some people believe that fables were stories told by poor people to express criticism of rich people. Others believe that fables were proverbs made into stories.

Whatever the case, a fable is simply a short story that teaches a lesson or moral. Sometimes the moral is actually written at the end of the story. Other times, the reader must determine what the lesson or moral is.

Fables have no fixed time or place, which may account for their popularity over hundreds of years. Quite often the characters in fables are animals that have taken on human characteristics.

THE FROG PRINCESS

by Elizabeth Isele

Synopsis
This is an interesting folk tale set during the time of the Russian Czars. A search is conducted to find the needle needed to kill Old Bones the Immortal.

Vocabulary

1. agony	7. drake	13. lopsided	19. outraged
2. bewildered	8. embroidered	14. maidens	20. rejoicing
3. convey	9. fates	15. magnificent	21. Russia
4. cunning	10. furious	16. miniature	22. summoned
5. czar	11. grieve	17. mocked	23. vain
6. despair	12. linen	18. nobleman	

Writing Activity
The needle needed to kill Old Bones the Immortal was hidden in an egg, which was in a duck, which was in a hare, which was kept in a chest. Have each student list four other items that could hold the needle and tell how this would change the story.

Curriculum Integration
Have the students find Russia on the map. Take the class to the library to find information about Russian czars.

Visuals
- Display pictures of Russia during the time of the czars.

I KNOW AN OLD LADY WHO SWALLOWED A FLY

by Nadine Bernard Westcott

Synopsis
This book is actually a folk song which has been put into story format and has been delightfully illustrated.

Vocabulary
1. absurd

Writing Activity
Students will enjoy completing the *"Fill In The Faces"* student page. Instruct the students to draw the details of the old lady's face at four different stages in the story and then to describe what is happening in each picture.

Curriculum Integration
In the story, the lady is a predator to insects and animals not normally preyed upon by humans. Have the students find the predators for each of the following:
1. fly
2. spider
3. bird
4. goat
5. horse

Have the students find out what these animals eat.
1. cat
2. dog
3. cow

Visuals
- Create a flannel board presentation to accompany the story.

FILL IN THE FACES

Draw the old lady's face as it would look at four stages in the story.
Then describe what is happening to make her look this way!

WHAT IS HAPPENING?

1.

2.

3.

4.

THE JOLLY POSTMAN

by Janet and Allan Ahlberg

Synopsis
The Jolly Postman rides his bicycle to deliver important pieces of mail to the Three Bears, the Wicked Witch, the Giant, Cinderella, the Big Bad Wolf, and Goldilocks.

Vocabulary
1. bloke
2. cackle
3. cease
4. glee
5. harassment
6. nightingales
7. occupying
8. porridge

Writing Activity
Ask each student to compose a letter, an invitation, or an advertisement to be mailed to a favorite story character.

Curriculum Integration
Help the students create a map of the journey of the Jolly Postman. They should show his travels from start to finish by drawing the characters' homes along the way.

Visuals
- Present the mail as it is found in the envelopes in the book.

ONCE A MOUSE

by Marcia Brown

Synopsis
This is the tale of a powerful but foolish hermit who is tricked into changing a mouse into a cat, then into a dog, and finally into a tiger. The hermit ultimately makes a foolish mistake.

Vocabulary
1. chided
2. gesture
3. hermit
4. humiliated
5. "lording it over"
6. offended
7. pride
8. prowling
9. stout
10. ungrateful
11. wretched

Writing Activity
The Hermit changes the mouse into a cat, then into a dog, and finally into a tiger. Ask the students to think of two additional ways that they could change the mouse. Let the students tell what would happen after each change. Use this format:

I would change the mouse into a

_____ .
        (1)

If the _____ met a
  (same as blank 1)

_____ ,

(other animal or creature)

I would change it into a _____ .
                (2)

Curriculum Integration
Once A Mouse received the Caldecott Award for its beautiful wood-print illustrations. The students may create pictures using linoleum blocks, potatoes, cardboard, etc. Each student may recreate a scene that he or she remembers from the story.

Have the students find India on the map. Ask the students to find two historical facts about India's people or culture.

Visuals
- Display pictures of India and/or the jungle.

THE PAPER CRANE

by Molly Bang

Synopsis

When a new highway replaces the old highway, a once prosperous restaurant rarely is visited anymore. The restaurant's owner willingly feeds a stranger who cannot pay and is repaid in a strange and delightful way.

Vocabulary

1. crane
2. gentle
3. host
4. overjoyed
5. stranger
6. unusual

Writing Activity

Have the students create "missing letter" stories about another adventure of the paper crane. First, students must decide what letter to omit from their stories. Then they must create their adventures. Each time a student comes to a word which has the "omitted" letter, he or she should leave a blank where the letter should be. For example: _fter the str_nger _nd the cr_ne flew _w_y, they _rrived _t _ sm_ll town in Minnesot_. (The missing letter is a.) Have the students display their stories for classmates to read and "solve."

Curriculum Integration

Have the students try origami. (The crane would be difficult for younger children, but a hat or ship would be easy to master.)

Let the students create cut-paper art projects such as the pictures found in the book.

Visuals

- origami examples
- the book's illustrations

SYLVESTER AND THE MAGIC PEBBLE

by William Steig

Synopsis
The old adage "Be careful what you wish for" rings true in this adventure. This book, filled with complex symbolism, has a message that will appeal to young and old alike.

Vocabulary
1. aimlessly	8. concluded	15. gully	21. remarkable
2. alfalfa	9. disappeared	16. inquiring	22. reminded
3. bewildered	10. dreadful	17. insisted	23. sassafras
4. bounding	11. existed	18. mysterious	24. shiver
5. ceased	12. extraordinary	19. panicked	25. soothe
6. collecting	13. fetlock	20. perplexed	

Writing Activity
Establish the following scenario for the students: "Suppose that Sylvester had been able to think more clearly when he was first confronted by the lion on Strawberry Hill. How would the magic pebble have changed his life and the lives of his family and friends if he had not become a stone? Would the pebble have brought them happiness or even greater sorrow?" Instruct the students to rewrite the story and illustrate a memorable portion of it.

Curriculum Integration
Help the students to establish a procedure for completing a book critique. Critiques should include the following information:
1. Give the title of the book.
2. Tell why you did or didn't like the book.
3. Who were the main characters? Describe them.
4. Was there a problem in the story? If so, how was it solved?
5. Did you like the ending? If not, how would you have changed it?

Students should critique one of Steig's other works using these criteria.

Visuals
- Steig's illustrations

STREGA NONA

by Tomie dePaola

Synopsis

This Caldecott Award winning story of a magical old lady named Strega Nona will keep all readers spellbound. Pasta expands and expands across the town as Big Anthony breaks a promise.

Vocabulary

1.	alas	5.	pasta
2.	barricade	6.	sputter
3.	convent	7.	town square

Writing Activity

Strega Nona was capable of curing several problems with her magic. She could cure a headache with oil, water and a hairpin. Have each student choose a problem he or she would like to cure and write a cure for it.

Students may want to write about a fair and just punishment for Big Anthony.

Curriculum Integration

Have the students find Italy on the map. Ask the students to find out something about the Italian culture and language.

Visuals

• Bring several kinds of pasta noodles to class for the students to examine, cook, and eat.

THE THIEF WHO HUGGED A MOONBEAM

by Harold Berson

Synopsis
When a local thief tries to outsmart one of the town's wealthy men, he finds out that he is an unlucky thief and a fool as well.

Vocabulary
1. confidence   4. moonbeam
2. greedy   5. successful
3. interrupted   6. whisked

Writing Activity
Have each student write a story telling how he or she could trick someone into doing something. (Who would you fool? What trick would you use?) Instruct each student to use two of the vocabulary words in the story.

You may wish to read only the middle of the story and have the students write their own beginnings and endings.

Curriculum Integration
This tale was originally written in Latin. Have the students find out something about Latin and why it is important to us today.

Each student might enjoy drawing a picture of his or her favorite part of the story. (The students should write captions beneath their illustrations.)

Visuals
- books of folklore
- the book's illustrations

THREE AESOP FOX FABLES

by Paul Galdone

Synopsis
These three classic fables will delight young readers.

Vocabulary
1. advice
2. appointed
3. crouched
4. exchange
6. lapped
7. lofty
8. marsh
9. quench
10. scorn
11. sipped
12. tempting

Writing Activity
Write the morals or lessons of the three stories on the board. Have the students write short, modern-day fables that convey these morals.

Have the students brainstorm a list of words that describe how people and animals eat (lap and sip, for example).

Curriculum Integration
Students may research to find factual information about the fox.

Have the students create lists of facts and fiction about the fox as presented in the fables. For example:

Fact
1. The fox is an animal.

Fiction
1. The fox can talk.

Visuals:
- pictures from the story

THE THREE SILLIES

by Paul Galdone

Synopsis
Little seems to make sense in this topsy-turvy tale in which a moon falls into a pond, a woman tries to make a cow climb a ladder, and a young man takes a silly for a bride. Children will delight in the unusual worries shared by these characters.

Vocabulary
1. beams
2. dreadful
3. horrid
4. insisted
5. reflection
6. trousers

Writing Activity
Have each student write answers to these questions: "If the book had been called *The Four Sillies*, who would the fourth silly be? What part would he or she play in the story?"

The young man's bride seems very silly, indeed. Have the students write about one of the silly things she would do after getting married.

Curriculum Integration
Have each student complete the *"Story Sequencing Wheel"* student page.

Visuals
- other books of fables or folklore
- the book's illustrations

Name _____

STORY SEQUENCING WHEEL

Write the events from the story *The Three Sillies* in order around the sequencing wheel.

The young gentleman pulled the ax from the beam.

The old woman tried to get the cow to climb the ladder.

"Whatever is the matter?" asked the father.

The young man ran as fast as he could.

The cow slid off the roof.

The other man tried to jump into his trousers.

The people said that the moon had fallen into the pond.

Everyone lived happily ever after.

The young man showed the other man how to put on his trousers.

The young man and the silly got married.

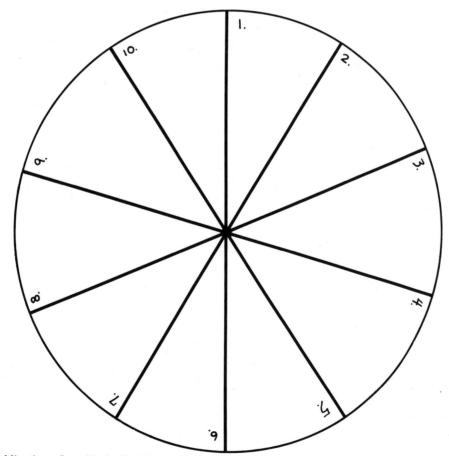

THE WILD WASHERWOMEN

by John Yeoman

Synopsis
The woes of the women who washed mountains of dirty laundry long ago are delightfully exaggerated in this folk tale.

Vocabulary
1. filthy
2. ghastly
3. grimy
4. marvelous
5. plunged
6. rampage
7. timidly

Writing Activity
Discuss the importance of adjectives to a story. Instruct the students to divide their papers into four sections and to list as many adjectives as they can for the words dirty, nice, tired, and clean. Have the students create word wheels for each word and its adjectives.

Ask each student to write about an invention that would help the washerwomen with their mountains of dirty laundry. The students should write about how their inventions work and then illustrate the inventions.

Curriculum Integration
Have the students work in groups of four to choose a modern-day invention and explain how it has changed our lives. Ask the students to consider how our lives might be different today if the invention did not exist.

Visuals
- Display pictures of timesaving inventions (to spark discussion about how inventions have changed our lives).

ALEXANDER AND THE TERRIBLE, HORRIBLE, NO GOOD, VERY BAD DAY

by Judith Viorst

Synopsis

Alexander experiences a dreadful day and the "audience" enjoys the humor of his misfortune. The repetition of the words, "I could tell it was going to be a terrible, horrible, no good, very bad day," will delight young readers.

Vocabulary

1. Australia
2. castle
3. dessert
4. elevator
5. horrible
6. invisible
7. mistake
8. sneakers
9. terrible
10. tongue

Writing Activity

Write this sentence on the board: "I could tell it was going to be a terrible, horrible, no good, very bad day." Have the students write real or imaginative stories about themselves or others following the same line of thinking. Students can add on to the sentence if they choose. For example: "I could tell it was going to be a terrible, horrible, no good, very bad day when _____."The students should illustrate their stories. Compile the stories to make a class book titled "Our Class And The Terrible, Horrible, No Good, Very Bad Day."

Curriculum Integration

Explore the book's illustrations. Allow the students to use body language to express emotions similar to those felt by Alexander.

Visuals

- Display additional books by Judith Viorst.

BLUEBERRIES FOR SAL

by Robert McCloskey

Synopsis
A young boy and a bear cub exchange mothers for an afternoon of humorous adventures. The mismatch is resolved in a peaceful manner.

Vocabulary
1. blueberries
2. bushes
3. clump
4. hustle
5. munching
6. struggled

Writing Activity
Ask each student to write a recipe from memory for a favorite food. Then have the students bring copies of the actual recipes to class. Compose a class recipe book of the "imaginative" and real recipes.

Curriculum Integration
Make blueberry muffins, or create one of the recipes from the class recipe book.

Recipe:
1/4 cup butter or margarine
1/2 cup sugar
1 egg
3/4 cup milk
3/4 cup flour
1/4 tsp. vanilla
2 1/2 tsp. baking powder
1/2 tsp. salt
1 cup blueberries

Cream butter and sugar until light and fluffy. Beat in egg and then milk and vanilla. Beat until nearly smooth. In a small bowl add together 3/4 cup flour, baking powder, and salt. Add to milk mixture; stir until moist. Toss in berries. Spoon into greased muffin tins. Bake at 425 degrees. While muffins are still hot, brush with butter and dip in sugar.

Visuals
• Display books by McCloskey and eat blueberries!

ENCYCLOPEDIA BROWN, BOY DETECTIVE

by Donald J. Sobol

Synopsis
LeRoy Brown and his detective agency are involved in the business of solving crimes. The stories contain humorous adventures and suspense for young readers.

Vocabulary
1.	advice	6.	league
2.	champion	7.	scattered
3.	collected	8.	sprained
4.	courtroom	9.	thief

Writing Activity
Form small groups to create detective agencies. Each agency will need a name and a mystery to solve. Give the students probable mystery titles to spark their creative interests. Then allow the students to write brief mystery plays and act them out as an agency.

Probable mystery titles might include:

The Case of the Missing Lunch Tickets
The Case of the Mystery Student Visitor
The Case of the Classroom Bully
The Case of the Disappearing Homework
The Case of the Torn Tennis Shoes

Curriculum Integration
Contact the Federal Bureau of Investigation or the local police department and invite a guest speaker to address the topic of crime prevention. The visitor may address additional topics such as safety for children.

Visuals
- Bring a fingerprinting kit to class and take each child's prints.

- Create a reading center filled with mystery books.

THE GIVING TREE

by Shel Silverstein

Synopsis
A young boy's joy is shown as he plays with his friend — a tree. We watch the boy grow older and encounter change in himself and the tree as well.

Vocabulary
1. crowns
2. forest
3. gathered
4. money
5. rest
6. sailed
7. swing
8. trunk

Writing Activity
Discuss the idea of change. Brainstorm as a group the things that change in our world. Chart how changes can be both positive and negative. Ask the students to classify the changes that have been named and to explain their reasons.

Curriculum Integration
Let the students create leaf prints!

Directions: Put leaves under lightweight paper. Rub the paper with a crayon or chalk.

Discuss various types of trees and the differences in their leaves.

Visuals
- Provide each child with a collection of leaves.

I KNOW A LADY

by Charlotte Zolotow

Synopsis
The beauty of the friendship between an older lady and a young girl is presented in a sensitive manner. The details of nature portrayed by the illustrations add to the peacefulness of this story.

Vocabulary
1. chrysanthemums
2. daffodils
3. meadow
4. sprinkled
5. zinnias

Writing Activity
Discuss how it would feel to live alone. The lady in the story remained nameless. Ask the students why they think the author chose not to give the lady a name. Discuss how the little girl felt about the lady in the story.

Brainstorm ideas about gifts that can be found in nature or that can be made by hand. Encourage each student to write a follow-up paragraph titled "The Most Precious Gift."

Curriculum Integration
Have each student create a book about flowers or nature. Students may create illustrations using a variety of media — watercolors, tempera paints, chalk, cut paper, etc.

Let each student choose a craft from a craft book and demonstrate it for the class.

Visuals
• Display craft books, nature books, and flower books.

LENTIL

by Robert McCloskey

Synopsis
Lentil receives a harmonica that starts an extraordinary chain of events in his life. The illustrations and unusual characters will delight the students.

Vocabulary
1. harmonica
2. improved
3. indignant
4. musicians
5. private
6. trombone
7. whittling

Writing Activity
Ask each student to create a list of ten wishes that are truly important to him or her. (Students may not make more than ten wishes.) Then ask the students to prioritize their lists and to choose one wish that could actually come true. Each student may share this wish with the group and explain what would be necessary in order for the wish to become a reality.

Curriculum Integration
Let the students experiment with harmonicas! (Each student will need his or her own harmonica.)

Visuals
- Display music books and additional books by Robert McCloskey.

LOUDMOUTH GEORGE AND THE SIXTH GRADE BULLY

by Nancy Carlson

Synopsis
An enormous sixth grader constantly harasses George on his way home from school. George's good friend Harriet assists George in solving the problem.

Vocabulary
1. attention
2. enormous
3. excited
4. garlic powder
5. squirt

Writing Activity
Discuss with the students how all people may experience problems during their lives. Let the students share experiences they have had that made them afraid. Give each student a copy of the *"A Problem To Solve"* student page. Instruct the students to choose a real or imaginary problem and to create a workable solution for the problem.

Curriculum Integration
Act out the scenes from the story in groups of three.

Visuals
• Display other books by Nancy Carlson.

Name _____

A PROBLEM TO SOLVE

Write a real or imaginary problem in the space below.
Then write a solution for the problem.

My Problem: _____

_____

_____

_____

_____

My Solution: _____

_____

_____

_____

_____

Illustrate the problem and solution.

MRS. PIGGLE WIGGLE

by Betty MacDonald

Synopsis
Mrs. Piggle Wiggle has magical wizardry skills. She solves problems in humorous ways that keep the reader giggling.

Vocabulary
1. apologized
2. buried
3. closets
4. examine
5. immaculate
6. politely
7. practice
8. soggy
9. squat
10. trimmed

Writing Activity
Ask the students this question: What would happen if Mrs. Piggle Wiggle were to spend the day at your house? Have the students write stories describing Mrs. Piggle Wiggle's actions.

Curriculum Integration
Let each student create a button to advertise the story of *Mrs. Piggle Wiggle*. Have the students wear their buttons to celebrate "Mrs. Piggle Wiggle Day."

Visuals
- Display additional books about Mrs. Piggle Wiggle.

RAMONA THE PEST

by Beverly Cleary

Synopsis
Ramona declares that she is not a pest as labeled by her sister Beezus Quimby. Interesting conversations occur between the girls as they tackle the world together.

Vocabulary
1. attention	4. defeat	7. marched	10. recognized
2. beamed	5. indignant	8. opinion	11. scowled
3. commotion	6. managed	9. principal	12. shoulders

Writing Activity
Discuss why humor is so important.

As a follow-up, ask the students to write advice to Ramona about what to do with Beezus (or to Beezus regarding what to do about Ramona).

Curriculum Integration
Have each student use a shoe box to create a three-dimensional doghouse for Ribsy. Students can make Ribsy by covering a short, elongated balloon with papier-mâché. Then have the students compose dialogue reflecting what Ribsy might be thinking during one of the girls' conversations.

Visuals
• Display additional Beverly Cleary books.

MISS RUMPHIUS

by Barbara Cooney

Synopsis

Alice Rumphius has two wishes in life — to travel the world and to live by the sea. When her grandfather tells her as a young girl that she also must do something to make the world more beautiful, she is not sure what that will be.

Vocabulary

1. bristling
2. conservatory
3. figureheads
4. jasmine
5. lupines

6. masts
7. prow
8. stoop
9. tropical isle
10. wharves

Writing Activity

Have the students complete these sentences: When I grow up, I would like to _____ and _____ . One thing that I could do to make the world more beautiful would be to _____ .

Curriculum Integration

Let the students plant different types of flower seeds and record observations every three days for three to four weeks. Discuss the growth as new observations are made.

Visuals

- pictures of lupines (or real ones, if possible)
- illustrations from the book (note: the illustrations were made in an interesting way which is noted on the last page of the book)

STEVIE

by John Steptoe

Synopsis
Stevie is a pesty youngster who comes into a family to live as a boarder. The family's boy resents the pest, but grows fond of him as the story progresses. Stevie tags along and messes up the boy's belongings.

Vocabulary
1. blamed
2. cousin
3. footprints
4. friends
5. nerves
6. remembered

Writing Activity
Discuss how younger children sometimes make older children angry or glad. Create "mad" and "glad" charts. The headings should read: I am mad when . . . ; I am glad when . . . .

Curriculum Integration
Have the students create "touch booklets" to give to younger children. Students may draw pictures in their booklets and glue objects with unusual textures to the pictures (sandpaper, satin, fur, etc.). The booklets may have story lines or they may simply be examples of tactile sensations. Encourage the students to share their finished products with younger children.

Visuals
• Display objects with unusual textures.

THROUGH GRANDPA'S EYES

by Patricia MacLacklan

Synopsis
A blind grandfather teaches his grandson about a positive view of life. The friendship between the grandfather and his grandson develops as they go exploring in nature.

Vocabulary
1. banister
2. bridge
3. carnations
4. cello
5. exercise
6. favorite
7. grumble
8. stretching

Writing Activity
Spend time discussing point of view. Ask each student to write a story from the point of view of a grandfather or grandmother. Each story needs to include an episode spent with younger children and the adventures that occur. Have the students sign their stories.

Curriculum Integration
Cover a student's eyes and let him or her walk around the room. (Do this for each student one at a time.) Discuss the reactions of the students. Invite a blind person to visit the class and talk about his or her way of life. (This story also can tie into a Grandparents' Day celebration.)

Visuals
- Display books written in Braille. (The Societies for the Blind have cards of Braille for students to keep.)

WHITE DYNAMITE AND THE CURLY KID

by Bill Martin Jr.

Synopsis

A rodeo serves as the setting for this story which describes a young child's adventures with his dad. The language twists and turns and gives a special effect to the dialogue between the dad and the child.

Vocabulary

1. bull
2. chew
3. corkscrew
4. dynamite
5. extra
6. perfect
7. rodeo
8. scared

Writing Activity

For a change of pace, have the students write stories in groups. The key focus of each story should be the dialogue. Ask the students to choose a circus, a ski resort, the mountains, or a campground for the setting of the story. The students in each group should delineate the character first and then input the dialogue of their individual characters.

Curriculum Integration

Encourage the students to create "academic rodeo contests." Students may come up with ideas such as the "rope your way to good spelling contest" in which the cowboys and cowgirls take turns placing small ropes around the correctly spelled words in a group. The students will enjoy creating interesting rodeo events.

Visuals

- Playing western music and making a fake campfire will provide a unique setting for the reading of this story.

APRIL FOOL!

by Leland B. Jacobs

Synopsis
Leland Jacobs has written a suspenseful April Fools' Day story that involves a young lady named Nancy. The reader will anticipate the next silly trick to come Nancy's way.

Vocabulary
1. blacksmith
2. brayed
3. candle maker
4. game warden
5. plough
6. tantrum
7. tax collector

Writing Activity
Have the students brainstorm activities that the king would find to be very foolish. Students may complete this sentence four times each:

It would be very foolish to _____ .

Curriculcum Integration
Challenge the students to discover the origin of April Fools' Day. (See Jacobs' note in this regard at the end of the book.)

Visuals
- Display pictures of medieval times, the Renaissance period, etc.

CHICKEN SALAD SOUP

by Alvin Granowsky and Joy and Craig Tweedt

Synopsis
A young boy wishes to surprise his family with a chicken soup recipe. He uses the computer to assist him in his planning. The results are disastrous!

Vocabulary
1. computer
2. mayonnaise
3. mistake
4. recipe

Writing Activity
Discuss how all people make mistakes and how learning to laugh at ourselves is very important. Instruct the students to write stories about someone's making a mistake. Remind them to add humor to their stories.

Curriculum Integration
Computers are very useful tools in our society. Have the students explore the different kinds of people who use computers to assist them in their daily tasks.

Visuals
- Create computer printouts (one for each student) of a recipe for chicken salad.
- Let the students eat chicken soup and crackers!

CHICKEN SOUP WITH RICE

by Maurice Sendak

Synopsis
The rhyming lines created by Maurice Sendak make *Chicken Soup With Rice* a delightful action-packed adventure through the seasons.

Vocabulary
1. anniversary
2. charm
3. crocodile
4. draped
5. slipping
6. spills
7. spout
8. sprinkle
9. twice

Writing Activity
Ask each student to choose his or her favorite month of the year and to design a chicken soup poem. The poem may end with the words, "chicken soup with rice." Encourage the students to illustrate their poems.

Curriculum Integration
Children may illustrate the seasons by creating watercolor pictures of their favorite "parts" of each season. Remind the students to title each painting.

Visuals
- Display additional books written by Maurice Sendak.

THE GIANT JAM SANDWICH

by John Vernon Lord and Janet Burroway

Synopsis
This hilarious adventure involves the production of a giant jam sandwich to rid the town of its wasps.

Vocabulary
1. dough
2. gentleman
3. instructions
4. nuisance
5. wasps

Writing Activity
Give each student a large sheet of light brown paper cut in the shape of a sandwich. Discuss the skills of elaboration (adding many details to a story) and exaggeration (the ability to make things bigger than life) as useful tools for writers. Instruct the students to write descriptions of their unusual sandwiches.

Curriculum Integration
Make a batch of no-cook strawberry jam. (Students will enjoy helping!)

Crush strawberries to measure 1 3/4 cup. In a bowl, stir strawberries with 3 cups sugar and 1 cup light corn syrup until blended. Let stand 10 minutes. Mix 2 (3 oz.) pouches of liquid fruit pectin and 2 tablespoons lemon juice. Blend this with the berries. Continue to mix for 3 minutes. Ladle jam into 1/2 pint freezer jars, leaving room for expansion. Cover tightly and place in the freezer to be used for up to three weeks.

Visuals
- Display pictures of spring trees and plants.
- Eat jam sandwiches together.
- Let the students examine a wasp's nest.

JAM

by Margaret Mahy

Synopsis
Mr. Castle's comic adventures during his first experience as a housefather involve making jam with his children. The more plums that fall, the faster the family must make their delicious jam.

Vocabulary
1. anxious
2. castle
3. medicine
4. scientist
5. thud

Writing Activity
Have the class brainstorm for words related in some way to the words "plum" and "castle." Write the words on the board using the "webbing" technique shown below. Then instruct the students to choose their own topics to "web."

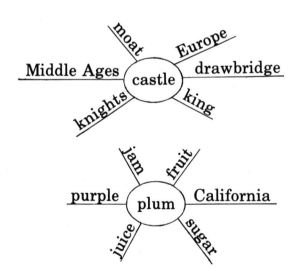

Curriculum Integration
Young jam makers will enjoy making the following recipe:

5 cups chopped plums
3 cups sugar
1 small pkg. raspberry gelatin dessert

Cut plums fine. Mix with sugar and cook until boiling for one minute. Stir in raspberry gelatin dessert. Spoon in glasses and refrigerate.

Visuals
- Display pictures of castles, kings, queens, and books about Europe.

THE POPCORN BOOK

by Tomie dePaola

Synopsis

Tony and Tiny are twin brothers who explore the making of popcorn from a historic viewpoint. The illustrations add an element of humor that blends beautifully with the warmth of the story.

Vocabulary

1. archeologist
2. colonists
3. Columbus
4. Indians
5. interest
6. kernels
7. sponsor

Writing Activity

Discuss with the class the difference between fact and opinion. Cite examples of each from the story. Have the students design "Popcorn Fact and Opinion" booklets. The booklets should include historic facts about the development of popcorn. In addition, students should add their own opinions about popcorn as well as those of friends or family.

Curriculum Integration

Help the students categorize different popcorn seeds according to color, texture, and size. Look for attributes that distinguish one kernel from another. Place the kernels in groups according to a chart created by the class.

Visuals

- Enjoy bowls of popcorn during the story.
- Examine Indian corn and domestic brands of popping corn.

STONE SOUP

by Marcia Brown

Synopsis
Three soldiers come to a town on their way home from war. In order to provide the soldiers with a nutritious meal, the peasants prepare a fancy stone soup that delights the visitors.

Vocabulary
1. barley
2. broth
3. cabbage
4. impossible
5. potatoes
6. soldiers
7. spare
8. torches

Writing Activity
Ask each student to choose one of the following story titles about which to write an original adventure:

The Day Soldiers Came To My Town
I Played A Trick
Adventures In An Old Village

Curriculum Integration
Let the class enjoy stone soup. Ask each student to bring a particular kind of vegetable from home (carrots, celery, onions, tomatoes, etc.). You may add meat if you like. Simmer the vegetables and meat for an hour and a half in three cups of water. Season to taste.

Visuals
• Share other Marcia Brown stories with the class.

ANNIE AND THE OLD ONE

by Miska Miles

Synopsis
Annie's Navajo world is permeated with her family and nature. The Old One teaches Annie many lessons about life. The skillful illustrations add to the sensitivity of this book.

Vocabulary
1. cactus
2. crisscrossed
3. harmony
4. hogan
5. Navajo
6. respect
7. scattered
8. warp
9. weaving
10. wrinkles

Writing Activity
The Old One taught Annie a lesson about life. Ask each student to write a paragraph about the lessons he or she has learned from older people. Let the students illustrate their paragraphs if they choose.

Curriculum Integration
Have the students construct weaving boards and use yarn to weave patterns. (The boards may be made of cardboard and strung with light-weight string.)

Let the students help to bake cornbread using the following recipe:

1 cup cornmeal
1 cup flour
2 tbsp. sugar
4 tsp. baking powder
1/4 tsp. salt
1 cup milk
1/4 cup shortening
1 egg

Preheat oven to 400 degrees. Mix all ingredients well. Pour into a greased loaf pan. Bake for approximately 25 minutes. Serve with honey or jam.

Invite a Native American speaker or a weaver to visit the class.

Visuals
- Display Native American art.
- Create a weaving center.

THE BIGGEST BEAR

by Lynd Ward

Synopsis

Johnny dreamed of having a bearskin rug. Johnny's parents were quite surprised when he arrived with a young cub on his shoulder. The problems of owning a fully grown bear make life difficult for Johnny.

Vocabulary

1. hardly
2. orchard
3. smokehouse
4. timber
5. warning

Writing Activity

Instruct each student to work through the problem-solving process in regards to this story.

1. Describe the problems that Johnny experienced in this story.
2. What are some possible solutions to those problems?
3. What criteria should Johnny use to decide which solutions are best?
4. Make a decision about the bear's future using the criteria.

Have the students use the problem-solving process with another story in which a problem is of paramount importance, or have the students use the process to solve a school problem.

Curriculum Integration

Discuss the value of a zoo or other animal preservation center in your area. Ask the students these questions: If you were in charge of animal preservation for your state, how would you choose to redesign the local zoo? What changes would you make and why? Ask the students to draw their new zoos.

Visuals

• Create a bear display.

THE GIRL WHO LOVED WILD HORSES

by Paul Goble

Synopsis

The young Native American girl's love for horses blossoms when she goes to live with them for two years. The horses move across each page in brilliant paintings surrounded by nature.

Vocabulary

1. admire
2. blizzards
3. courage
4. daybreak
5. herds
6. mare
7. meadows
8. scent
9. stallion

Writing Activity

Paul Goble has filled his story with action words. Let the class list some of the action words from the story on a large chart. As the students try to visualize the action words, encourage them to write action-packed sentences, each containing four or five related action words. Instruct each student to develop his or her sentences into a paragraph that could have been pulled out of an imaginary story. (Have the students illustrate their action-packed sentences.)

Curriculum Integration

Instruct each student to create a nature scene (mountains, a valley, a meadow, a lake, or a prairie) using watercolors.

Allow the students to use a stencil to create black construction paper horses (or students may free-form the horses). Students may glue the horse silhouettes against their watercolor nature scenes and frame their scenes with construction paper.

Visuals

• Display books about horses.

THE GLORIOUS FLIGHT: ACROSS THE CHANNEL WITH LOUIS BLERIOT

by Alice and Martin Provensen

Synopsis
This historic account of Louis Bleriot's flight across the English Channel will delight young readers.

Vocabulary

1. aeronaut
2. beneath
3. bruised
4. glorious
5. lever
6. propellers
7. shiny
8. signal
9. splash

Writing Activity
Louis Bleriot had a dream of inventing an airplane and flying across the English Channel. He accomplished his dream by using his determination and creative ideas. Ask each student to pretend to invent a machine that allows him or her to travel and to tell the class about the invention in great detail. Encourage the students to write adventures about their new machines and to illustrate their stories.

Curriculum Integration
Invite the students to bring to class models of transportation vehicles that they have made. Set up a center for model building. Furnish the center with several models that the students may complete in small groups during their free time.

Discuss the importance of following directions when completing projects and the need for patience when working as a group.

Visuals
- Create a display of books concerning all types of transportation.
- Display models.

HEY, AL

by Arthur Yorinks

Synopsis
Al, a janitor, and his best friend, a dog named Eddie, enjoy a wonderful trip to paradise.

Vocabulary
1. fade
2. faithful
3. furious
4. growled
5. island
6. shimmering
7. struggle

Writing Activity
Discuss the lessons Al and Eddie learned from their adventure. Ask the students to write about a trip to an imaginary place. Remind the students that any animals in their stories should act like humans and should express feelings.

Curriculum Integration
Have each student make a collage of "paradise" using cut paper. Large tropical birds can be created using two large pieces of colorful paper. Students may cut feathers from brightly colored tissue paper and attach them to their birds.

Give each student a copy of the birdhouse instructions (see next page). Let the students work in small groups to build birdhouses. Supervise and assist the students as necessary. Encourage the students to investigate the proper ways to care for and feed wild birds.

Visuals
• Display pictures of birds.

EASY BIRDHOUSES TO MAKE

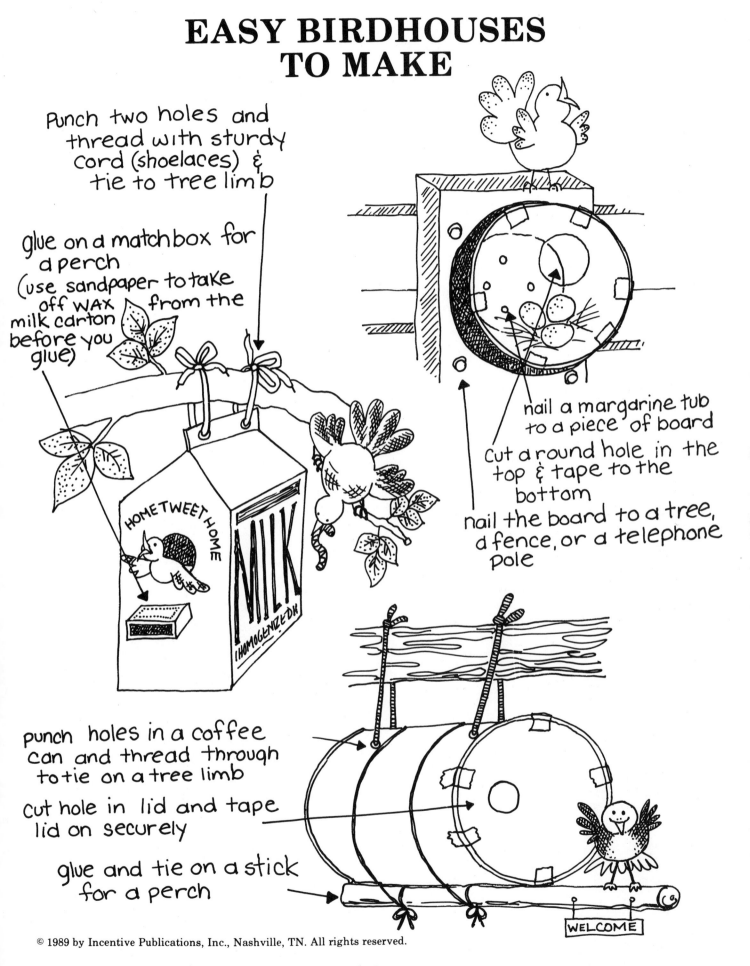

Punch two holes and thread with sturdy cord (shoelaces) & tie to tree limb

glue on a matchbox for a perch (use sandpaper to take off WAX from the milk carton before you glue)

HOME TWEET HOME

MILK (HOMOGENIZED)

nail a margarine tub to a piece of board

Cut a round hole in the top & tape to the bottom

nail the board to a tree, a fence, or a telephone pole

punch holes in a coffee can and thread through to tie on a tree limb

cut hole in lid and tape lid on securely

glue and tie on a stick for a perch

WELCOME

MADELINE'S RESCUE

by Ludwig Bemelmans

Synopsis
This Caldecott Award winning story takes place in Paris, France. A young girl, Madeline, is rescued by a dog and is taken to a convent for young girls.

Vocabulary
1. disaster
2. disgrace
3. frighten
4. inspection
5. noble
6. riot
7. sorrow
8. trustees
9. vines

Writing Activity
Each young writer should choose a country for the setting of a rescue story. Provide the students with resource books about many countries. (The rescue stories may include pets if the authors would like to follow the pattern of *Madeline's Rescue.*)

Curriculum Integration
Instruct each student to research a European country and to design a travel log pamphlet to share with an audience. (Display examples from a local travel bureau.) Allow each student to give a sales pitch for his or her chosen country.

Teach the students a few French words:
1. école (school)
2. nez (nose)
3. enfant (child)
4. stylo (pen)
5. uneauto (car)

Visuals
- Display a map of Europe and pictures of Paris.

MAKE WAY FOR DUCKLINGS

by Robert McCloskey

Synopsis
A mallard family creates a commotion as it travels through the city of Boston.

Vocabulary

1. cozy
2. enormous
3. hatch
4. molt
5. opposite
6. public
7. responsibility
8. scooters
9. squawked
10. suited

Writing Activity
Let each student design a poster to advertise the arrival of the ducklings. Then have the students write persuasive ads to protect an endangered animal. Discuss these questions: How can the public become more aware of the plight of endangered animals? What can people do once they become aware of the problem? How can you help to preserve our wildlife?

Curriculum Integration
Invite the students to illustrate some of the ducklings in the story. Students may add real duck feathers to their pictures!

Visuals
- You may want to write in advance to the Department of Natural Resources to ask for a list of endangered animals.
- Give each child a feather before reading the story.

OX-CART MAN

by Donald Hall

Synopsis
Students will enjoy experiencing nineteenth century life on a New England farm. The value of family members sharing in work and play is expressed uniquely by Donald Hall.

Vocabulary
1. barrel
2. carved
3. harness
4. sap
5. shawl
6. spinning wheel
7. turnips
8. yoke

Writing Activity
Have each student use the *"Past or Present?"* student page to list facts about life today and life in the nineteenth century. Have the students answer the questions on the student page and then discuss their answers.

Curriculum Integration
Help the students decorate jar lids to be placed on small jars of peppermint candy.

Visuals
- Let the students enjoy peppermint candy as they listen to the story.
- Display books about the nineteenth century.

Name _____

PAST OR PRESENT?

1. List facts about life today and life in the 19th century in the chart below.

Today	19th Century

2. Which time period, the 19th century or the present, do you think would be a better time in which to live and why? _____

_____

_____

3. If you could choose one thing about the present world that you would like to change, what would it be and why? _____

_____

_____

SAM, BANGS, AND MOONSHINE

by Evaline Ness

Synopsis
This is a sensitive book about a young girl who has trouble separating truth from "moonshine." Moonshine is the make-believe world that the young girl shares with her friends.

Vocabulary
1. curious
2. harbor
3. hollered
4. mermaid
5. scoured

Writing Activity
Sam has a habit of making up stories that are not true. Her father describes the stories as "moonshine." Discuss the skill of exaggeration. Then ask each student to write and illustrate a story with a little "moonshine." (Remind the students to concentrate on the details involved in defining a character for an audience.)

Curriculum Integration
Work as a class to create a bulletin board displaying the students' favorite animals or pets. The students may contribute photographs, newspaper or magazine clippings, poems, or other memorabilia.

Help the class find out as much as possible about the local animal shelter. Ask the students to answer these questions: What can we do to minimize the need for local animal shelters? What should shelters do with unwanted pets?

Visuals
- Display books and pictures about waterfronts, ships, and oceans.

WHERE THE WILD THINGS ARE

by Maurice Sendak

Synopsis
A young boy has a marvelous adventure with imaginative wild creatures. His mother sends him to his room where he takes control of the "wild things."

Vocabulary
1. ceiling
2. claws
3. mischief
4. private
5. rumpus

Writing Activity
The wild creatures in this story have unusual features. Ask the students to design their own imaginary wild things and to write brief dialogues between themselves and the wild things.

Curriculum Integration
Allow each student to design a special crown to wear for a "special" portion of the day.

Visuals
- Decorate a bulletin board with pictures of kings and queens.
- Display books about jungle animals.

THE AMINAL

by Lorna Balian

Synopsis

Patrick was having a picnic by himself when he decided to capture the "aminal" and be its friend. After giving the "aminal" a home in his lunch bag, he describes his new-found companion to his friend. As his friends redescribe Patrick's "aminal" to one another, their imaginations create a slightly different "aminal" each time. Soon they begin to fear for Patrick's safety. The unveiling of the "aminal" is heartwarming.

Vocabulary

1. breathlessly
2. dreadful
3. fig bars
4. gulped
5. offered
6. protected
7. quivered
8. squirmed

Writing Activity

Before reading the last three pages of the story, have the students write and illustrate their own endings. Let the students share their endings with the class before you read the actual ending.

Curriculum Integration

Cut out magazine pictures of various animals. Let each student choose a partner. Give one partner a picture of an animal. Instruct that partner to give clues to the other partner describing what the animal looks like. The second partner tries to draw the animal as it is described. Let the students share the results with the class.

Visuals

- Balian's illustrations

BRAVE IRENE

by William Steig

Synopsis

Brave Irene is a young heroine in every sense. Irene overcomes dangerous obstacles to deliver a dress to the duchess on behalf of her mother.

Vocabulary

1. aristocrats
2. cautioned
3. cherished
4. coaxed
5. delirious
6. duchess
7. errand
8. flounced
9. fret
10. furrows
11. hastening
12. helter-skelter
13. managed
14. moment
15. muffler
16. ordinary
17. plodding
18. pounced
19. radiant
20. splendid
21. squinting
22. strode
23. trudge
24. walloped
25. woe
26. wrenched

Writing Activity

The wind is a valuable yet sometimes frightening natural force. Brainstorm a list of ways in which the wind is helpful and a list of ways in which the wind is harmful. Ask the students to write mini-adventures about the wind. The class may wish to create a word wheel of "windy" words before beginning their stories.

Curriculum Integration

Instruct the students to conduct personal interviews with peers and adults in order to compile the following lists:

1. things that are more fun to do when it's windy
2. things that are less fun to do when it's windy

Encourage the students to hypothesize as to which topic will gather the greatest number of responses.

Visuals

- Create a windy story setting by using a fan.

DOCTOR DeSOTO

by William Steig

Synopsis
Dr. DeSoto, a renown dentist in the animal kingdom, finds himself in an ironic situation when he agrees to treat his enemy the fox.

Vocabulary

1. bitterly
2. caressed
3. chortled
4. clenched
5. dainty
6. delicate
7. extractor
8. gauze
9. hoisted
10. misery
11. morsel
12. particle
13. patient
14. permeate
15. pitiful
16. preparation
17. quiver
18. shabby
19. unique
20. winch
21. woozy

Writing Activity
Assist the students in creating a newspaper advertisement to sell the services of Dr. DeSoto to a new community of animals. Have the ad specifically detail his service and the importance of it. Make newspaper ads available for the students to use as examples.

Allow the students to express their concerns about dentists from "the patient's point of view."

Curriculum Integration
Create a set of animal fact and opinion cards by cutting pictures out of magazines and gluing the pictures on tagboard squares. On each card, write a sentence about the animal that is either factual or fictional. Then ask the students to conduct research to find out which cards state facts and which cards state opinions.

Visuals
• Steig's illustrations

THE GARDEN OF ABDUL GASAZI

by Chris Van Allsburg

Synopsis
Alan cannot decide if magic has been performed by an evil magician or if reality has somehow become impossible to explain. This is a thought-provoking adventure about a boy, a dog, and an unusual garden.

Vocabulary

1. absolutely	6. captured	11. midair
2. apologized	7. convinced	12. parlor
3. approached	8. dashing	13. positively
4. bellowed	9. detest	14. tremendous

Writing Activity
Have the students respond to the following question: "If You were thought to be the town magician and could only perform one magic trick, what would it be and why?" Ask each student to draw the house and gardens in which he or she would live.

Curriculum Integration
Van Allsburg's illustrations resemble lithographs, but all were done with carbon pencil. Students will enjoy creating pictures with carbon pencil. Discuss perspective as it relates to the artwork in the book.

Visuals
- lithographs
- other Van Allsburg books

THE HATING BOOK

by Charlotte Zolotow

Synopsis
This is a charming story of how children can quickly change their minds about "hate hating" their friends and can quickly forgive and forget.

Vocabulary
1. rather

Writing Activity
Ask students to complete these sentences and to illustrate their ideas:

When I am all alone I can _____

_____

_____ .

But I need a friend to _____

_____

_____ .

Example 1
When I am all alone I can run.
But I need a friend to race with me.

Example 2
When I am all alone I can swing.
But I need a friend to push me.

Curriculum Integration
Encourage the students to create their own "Hating Books" by answering the following questions.

1. What vegetable do you hate to eat?
2. What color do you hate to wear?
3. What sport do you hate to watch?
4. What chores do you hate to do at home?
5. What kind of pet would you hate to have?
6. What kind of competition would you hate to lose?
7. What kind of animal would you hate to meet in the jungle?
8. What kind of new food would you hate to try?

Counter this activity by having the students make "Loving Books."

Visuals
• Create a display of things you love and hate. Have the students guess what the items mean to you.

IMOGENE'S ANTLERS

by David Small

Synopsis
On Thursday morning, Imogene awakens to discover that she has grown antlers. While trying to resolve the problem, Imogene, the cook, and the maid find interesting uses for the antlers and try to make the best of the situation.

Vocabulary
1. antlers
2. bravissimo
3. bravo
4. consulted
5. decked
6. eventful
7. glared
8. milliner
9. overjoyed
10. prodded
11. thud
12. viola
13. wandered

Writing Activity
Have the students brainstorm for additional ideas about how Imogene's antlers could be useful if she were "stuck with them" for a period of time. Give each student a copy of the antler pattern on the following page to use in an oral presentation of his or her ideas.

Ask the students to engage in creative problem solving in order to determine ways that a peacock's tail could be used to "make the most of" an unusual situation. Encourage the students to write about and illustrate their ideas.

Curriculum Integration
Ask each student to compile a list of all the animals he or she can think of that have antlers. Students may wish to graph the different kinds of animals by continent. Have the students find out if any extinct animals had antlers.

Visuals
- Wear antlers as you read the story!

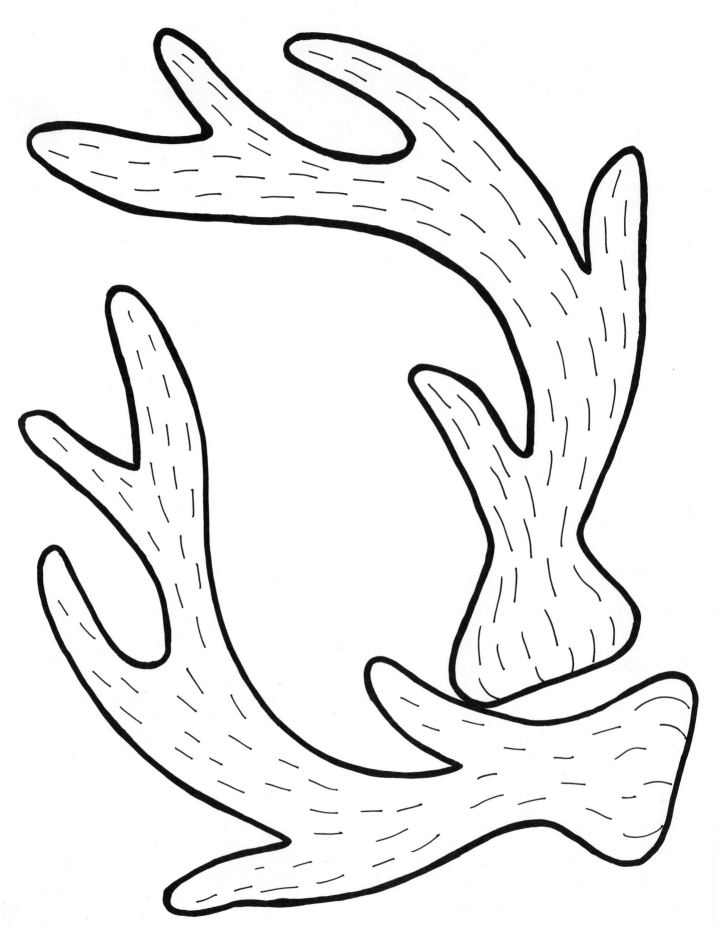

SIDNEY RELLA AND THE GLASS SNEAKERS

by Bernice Myers

Synopsis
The traditional glass slipper has been replaced by the glass sneaker in this modern-day Cinderella tale.

Vocabulary

1. corporation
2. insisted
3. manufacturers
4. mayor
5. stock market
6. uniform

Writing Activity
Discuss the similarities between Cinderella and Sidney Rella and chart the comparisons. Allow the students to choose another fairy tale that they like. Have pairs of students create their own "fractured fairy tales." The following chart will help the students create their stories.

Original Title	New Title
Original Characters	New Characters
Original Setting	New Setting
Original Adventures	New Adventures
Original Ending	New Ending

Have the students illustrate and share their stories.

Curriculum Integration
Instruct the students to "investigate" to find: 1) as many different versions of Cinderella as possible; 2)how many different countries have their own Cinderella tales. Ask each student to read another Cinderella version to a friend.

Visuals
• Create a display of fairy tales, football uniforms, sneakers, and different versions of Cinderella.

TIKKI TIKKI TEMBO

by Arlene Mosel

Synopsis
Chinese tradition dictates that the oldest child shall be given a long and grandiose first name. All other children born to a Chinese family are to be given shorter, less important names. In this story, this tradition is changed when the oldest child nearly drowns as a result of his long name.

Vocabulary
1. bewitched
2. glittering
3. heir
4. honored
5. miserable
6. mist
7. possess
8. reverence
9. rice cakes
10. tiresome

Writing Activity
Tikki Tikki Tembo's name has a musical, rhythmic quality. Let the students enjoy creating lengthy, rhythmic and musical names. Ask the students to illustrate the characters that would be given these names.

Curriculum Integration
Students may wish to find out more about:
1. the festival of the eighth moon
2. other Chinese holidays

Visuals
- Allow the students to sample rice cakes before or after the story.

234

THE VELVETEEN RABBIT

by Margery Williams

Synopsis
The Velveteen Rabbit is an endearing tale about a young boy's love for a toy. The rabbit becomes "real" as he shares the sad and joyous moments of the boy's life.

Vocabulary
1. boast
2. bracken
3. brigands
4. charming
5. commonplace
6. disabled
7. dreadful
8. expression
9. insignificant
10. mainspring
11. mantelpiece
12. mechanical
13. modern
14. parcels
15. rustling
16. scarlet fever
17. snubbed
18. splendid
19. sprig
20. succession
21. tidying up
22. wedged

Writing Activity
Ask each student to write a typical dialogue that could have taken place between the boy and the rabbit. Have the students illustrate their dialogues. Then have the students use the rabbit and boy finger puppets to "present" their dialogues.

Curriculum Integration
Ask the students to elaborate on this statement: "Friends are not always people."

Students may create their own "non-person" friends using dough made from 1 cup flour, 1/2 cup salt and 1/2 to 3/4 cup water. Students may color the dough with food coloring. Bake at 275 degrees for one hour or more depending on the thickness of the pieces.

Visuals
- Bring a "non-person" friend of yours to share with the class (stuffed animal, pet, etc.).
- Pass around a piece of velveteen fabric.

Cut along the dotted lines.
Insert fingers through holes.

BIBLIOGRAPHY

Alexander and the Terrible, Horrible, No Good, Very Bad Day, Judith Viorst. Macmillan, 1972.
Alexander and the Wind-Up Mouse, Leo Lionni. Knopf, Inc., 1987.
Amanda and the Witch Switch, John Himmelman. Viking, 1985.
The Amazing Pig, Paul Galdone. Houghton Mifflin, 1981.
The Aminal, Lorna Balian. Abingdon, 1985.
Animals Should Definitely Not Wear Clothing, Judi Barrett. Atheneum, 1970.
Annie and the Old One, Miska Miles. Little, Brown & Co. in association with the Atlantic Monthy Press, 1971.
April Fool! Leland B. Jacobs. Garrard, 1973.
Arthur's Christmas, Marc Brown. Little, Brown & Co., 1985.
Arthur's Halloween, Marc Brown. Little, Brown & Co., 1982.
Arthur's Nose, Marc Brown. Little, Brown & Co., 1982.
Arthur's Thanksgiving, Marc Brown. Little Brown & Co., 1982.
The Baby Uggs Are Hatching, Jack Prelutsky. Greenwillow Books, 1982.
Bah! Humbug? Lorna Balian. Abingdon, 1982.
Bea and Mr. Jones, Amy Schwartz. Bradbury Press, 1982.
Bear Shadow, Frank Asch. Prentice Hall, 1985.
Bee My Valentine, Miriam Cohen. Dell, 1983.
Begin at the Beginning, Amy Schwartz. Harper & Row Jr. Books, 1983.
Best Friends, Steven Kellogg. Dial Books for Young Readers, 1986.
The Best Valentine in the World, Marjorie Sharmat. Holiday House, 1982.
Big Bad Bruce, Bill Peet. Houghton Mifflin, 1978.
The Biggest Bear, Lynd Ward. Houghton Mifflin, 1973.
Big Mose: Hero Fireman, Harold W. Felton. Garrard, 1969.
The Big Orange Splot, Daniel M. Pinkwater. Scholastic, 1977.
Blueberries for Sal, Robert McCloskey. Penguin, 1976.
The Book of Pigericks, Arnold Lobel. Harper & Row Jr. Books. 1983.
Brave Irene, William Steig. Farrar, Strauss & Giroux, Inc., 1986.
The Brothers Wrong and Wrong Again, Louis Phillips. McGraw Hill, 1979.
Bubba and Babba, Maria Polushkin. Crown, 1986.
Can I Keep Him? Steven Kellogg. Dial Books for Young Readers, 1976.
A Chair for My Mother, Vera B. Williams. Greenwillow Books, 1982.
Chester the Worldly Pig, Bill Peet. Houghton Mifflin, 1978.
Chicken Salad Soup, Alvin Granowsky and Joy and Craig Tweedt. Modern Curriculum Press, 1985.
Chicken Soup with Rice, Maurice Sendak. Harper & Row Jr. Books, 1962.
A Chocolate Moose for Dinner, Fred Gwynne. Prentice Hall, 1987.
The Christmas Cat, Efner T. Holmes. Harper & Row Jr. Books, 1976.
The Cobweb Christmas, Shirley Climo. Harper & Row Jr. Books, 1986.
The Country Bunny and the Little Gold Shoes, DuBose Heyward. Houghton Mifflin, 1939.
Cranberry Christmas, Wende and Harry Devlin. Macmillan, 1980.
Cranberry Halloween, Wende and Harry Devlin. Macmillan, 1985.
Cranberry Thanksgiving, Wende and Harry Devlin. Macmillan, 1980.
The Day Jimmy's Boa Ate the Wash, Trinka H. Noble. Pied Piper Books, 1980.
Demi's Find the Animal ABC, Demi. Putnam Publishing Group, 1985.
Doctor DeSoto, William Steig. Farrar, Strauss & Giroux, Inc., 1982.
Don't Forget the Bacon, Pat Hutchins. Greenwillow, 1976.
Dorrie and the Goblin, Patricia Coombs. Lothrop, Lee & Shepard Co., 1972.
The Dream Eater, Christian Garrison. Macmillan, 1986.
The Easter Pig, Louise McClenathan. Morrow, 1982.
Encyclopedia Brown, Boy Detective, Donald J. Sobol. Lodestar Books, 1963.
Fables, Arnold Lobel. Harper & Row Jr. Books, 1980.
Freckles and Willie, Margery Cuyler. H. Holt & Co., 1986.
The Frog Princess, Elizabeth Isele. Harper & Row Jr. Books, 1984.
The Garden of Abdul Gasazi, Chris Van Allsburg. Houghton Mifflin, 1979.
The Giant Jam Sandwich, John V. Lord and Janet Burroway. Houghton Mifflin, 1973.
The Girl Who Loved Wild Horses, Paul Goble. Bradbury Press, 1978.
The Giving Tree, Shel Silverstein. Harper & Row Jr. Books, 1964.
The Glorious Flight: Across the Channel with Louis Bleriot, Alice and Martin Provensen. Penguin, 1987.
Grandpa's Farm, James Flora. Harcourt, Brace & World, 1965.
The Great Big Especially Beautiful Easter Egg, James Stevenson. Scholastic, Inc., 1987.
The Great Green Turkey Creek Monster, James Flora. Macmillan, 1976.

The Great Valentine's Day Balloon Race, Adrienne Adams. Macmillan, 1980.
Gregory the Terrible Eater, Mitchell Sharmat. Macmillan, 1980.
The Halloween Pumpkin Smasher, Judith St. George. Putnam Publishing Group, 1978.
Harriet's Halloween Candy, Nancy Carlson. Carolrhoda Books, 1982.
Harry and the Terrible Whatzit, Dick Gackenbach. Ticknor & Fields, 1984.
The Hating Book, Charlotte Zolotow. Harper & Row Jr. Books, 1969.
Helga High-Up, Marjorie Sharmat. Scholastic, 1988.
Herbie's Troubles, Carol Chapman. Dutton, 1981.
Hey, Al, Arthur Yorinks. Farrar, Strauss & Giroux, Inc., 1986.
Hubert's Hair-Raising Adventure, Bill Peet. Houghton Mifflin, 1979.
Humbug Witch, Lorna Balian. Abingdon, 1965.
If I Were In Charge of the World, Judith Viorst. Atheneum, 1981.
If You Give a Mouse a Cookie, Laura J. Numeroff. Harper & Row Jr. Books, 1985.
I Know a Lady, Charlotte Zolotow. Greenwillow Books, 1984.
I Know an Old Lady Who Swallowed a Fly, Nadine B. Westcott. The Atlantic Monthly Press, 1980.
Imogene's Antlers, David Small. Macmillan, 1987.
I'm Telling You Now, Judy Delton. Dutton, 1983.
I'm Terrific, Marjorie Sharmat. Holiday House, 1977.
Ira Sleeps Over, Bernard Waber. Houghton Mifflin, 1972.
The Island of the Skog, Steven Kellogg. Dial Books for Young Readers, 1976.
It Wasn't My Fault, Helen Lester. Houghton Mifflin, 1985.
It's Thanksgiving, Jack Prelutsky. Greenwillow Books, 1982.
I Was A Second Grade Werewolf, Daniel M. Pinkwater. Dutton, 1983.
I Will Not Go to Market Today, Harry Allard. Dial Press, 1979.
Jam, Margaret Mahy. The Atlantic Monthly Press, 1986.
Joey Runs Away, Jack Kent. Prentice Hall, 1985.
John Henry and Paul Bunyan Play Baseball, Wyatt Blassingame. Garrard, 1971.
The Jolly Postman, Janet and Allan Ahlberg. Little, Brown & Co., 1986.
Jumanji, Chris Van Allsburg. Houghton Mifflin, 1981.
King Wacky, Dick Gackenbach. Crown, 1984.
Lentil, Robert McCloskey. Viking, 1940.
Leprechauns Never Lie, Lorna Balian. Abingdon, 1980.
The Leprechaun's Story, Richard Kennedy. Dutton, 1979.
Louanne Pig in the Perfect Family, Nancy Carlson. Penguin, 1986.
Loudmouth George and the Sixth Grade Bully, Nancy Carlson. Penguin, 1985.
The Luckiest One of All, Bill Peet. Houghton Mifflin, 1982.
Madeline's Christmas, Ludwig Bemelmans. Viking, 1985.
Madeline's Rescue, Ludwig Bemelmans. Penguin, 1977.
The Magnificent Moo, Victoria Forrester. Macmillan, 1983.
Make Way for Ducklings, Robert McCloskey. Penguin, 1976.
Maude and Sally, Nicki Weiss. Greenwillow Books, 1983.
McBroom and the Big Wind, Sid Fleishman. The Atlantic Monthly Press, 1982.
Miss Nelson is Missing, Harry Allard and James Marshall. Houghton Mifflin, 1977.
Miss Rumphius, Barbara Cooney. Viking, 1982.
Mister Gaffe, see *The Queen of Eene*
Mother Told Me So, Carrol A. Marron. Raintree, 1983.
Mrs. Gaddy and the Fast-Growing Vine, Wilson Gage. Greenwillow, 1985.
Mrs. Minetta's Car Pool, Elizabeth Spurr. Macmillan, 1985.
Mrs. Peloki's Snake, Joanne Oppenheim. Dodd, 1980.
Mrs. Piggle Wiggle, Betty MacDonald. Harper & Row Jr. Books, 1957.
My Friend Jacob, Lucille Clifton. Dutton, 1980.
My Mom Hates Me In January, Judy Delton. Whitman, 1977.
The Mysterious Valentine, Nancy Carlson. Carolrhoda Books, 1985.
Nosey Mrs. Rat, Jeffrey Allen. Penguin, 1987.
No Such Things, Bill Peet. Houghton Mifflin, 1983.
Once A Mouse, Marcia Brown. Macmillan, 1982.
One Terrific Thanksgiving, Marjorie W. Sharmat. Holiday House, 1985.
One Tough Turkey, Steven Kroll. Holiday House, 1982.

The Other Emily, Gibbs Davis. Houghton Mifflin, 1984.
Ox-Cart Man, Donald Hall. Viking, 1979.
The Paper Crane, Molly Bang. Greenwillow, 1985.
The Patchwork Quilt, Valerie Flourney. Dial Books for Young Readers, 1985.
Pecos Bill Catches a Hidebehind, Wyatt Blassingame. Garrard, 1977.
Pelican, Brian Wildsmith. Pantheon, 1983.
Pig Pig Goes to Camp, David McPhail. Dutton, 1983.
The Pinkish, Purplish, Bluish Egg, Bill Peet. Houghton Mifflin, 1984.
The Polar Express, Chris Van Allsburg. Houghton Mifflin, 1984.
The Popcorn Book, Tomie dePaola. Holiday House, 1978.
The Queen of Eene, Jack Prelutsky. Greenwillow Books, 1978.
Ralph's Secret Weapon, Steven Kellogg. Dial Books for Young Readers, 1983.
Ramona the Pest, Beverly Cleary. Morrow, 1968.
The Relatives Came, Cynthia Rylant. Bradbury Press, 1985.
Rolling Harvey Down the Hill, Jack Prelutsky. Greenwillow Books, 1980.
Rosie and Michael, Judith Viorst. Atheneum, 1974.
Sam, Bangs and Moonshine, Evaline Ness. H. Holt & Co., 1966.
The Sheriff of Rottenshot, Jack Prelutsky. Greenwillow Books, 1982.
Sidney Rella and the Glass Sneakers, Bernice Myers. Macmillan, 1985.
Some Things Go Together, Charlotte Zolotow. Harper & Row Jr. Books, 1983.
Sometimes It's Turkey, Sometimes It's Feathers, Lorna Balian. Abingdon, 1986.
Stevie, John Steptoe. Harper & Row Jr. Books, 1986.
Stone Soup, Marcia Brown. Aladdin Books, 1986.
The Story of Ferdinand, Munro Leaf. Viking, 1936.
Strega Nona, Tomie dePaola. Treehouse, 1975.
A Sweetheart for Valentine, Lorna Balian. Abingdon, 1979.
Sylvester and the Magic Pebble, William Steig. Windmill Books, 1969.
Take Another Look, Tana Hoban. Greenwillow Books, 1981.
Tangles, Nancy Polette. Book Lures, 1983.
The Teeny-Tiny Woman, Paul Galdone. Ticknor & Fields, 1986.
Thanksgiving at the Tappleton's, Eileen Spinelli. Harper & Row Jr. Books, 1984.
Thanksgiving Day, Gail Gibbons. Holiday House, 1983.
That Dreadful Day, James Stevenson. Greenwillow Books, 1985.
The Thief Who Hugged a Moonbeam, Harold Berson. Seabury Press, 1972.
There's Nothing To Do! James Stevenson. Greenwillow Books, 1986.
Things To Make and Do for Thanksgiving, Lorinda Bryan Cauley. Watts, 1977.
Three Aesop Fox Fables, Paul Galdone. Seabury Press, 1971.
The Three Hundred Twenty-Ninth Friend, Marjorie Sharmat. Macmillan, 1979.
The Three Sillies, Paul Galdone. Houghton Mifflin, 1981.
Through Grandpa's Eyes, Patricia MacLacklan. Harper & Row Jr. Books, 1980.
Tikki Tikki Tembo, Arlene Mosel. Scholastic, Inc., 1984.
Today Was a Terrible Day, Patricia R. Giff. Penguin, 1984.
Unriddling, Alvin Schwartz. Harper & Row Jr. Books, 1983.
The Valentine Bears, Eve Bunting. Houghton Mifflin, 1985.
A Valentine for Cousin Archie, Barbara Williams. Dutton, 1981.
The Vanishing Pumpkin, Tony Johnston. Putnam Publishing Group, 1984.
The Velveteen Rabbit, Margery Williams. Messner, 1983.
Wake Up, Groundhog, Carol Cohen. Crown, 1977.
What's Under My Bed? James Stevenson. Greenwillow Books, 1983.
Where's Waldo? Martin Handford. Little, Brown & Co., 1987.
Where the Wild Things Are, Maurice Sendak. Harper & Row Jr. Books, 1984.
The Whingdingdilly, Bill Peet. Houghton Mifflin, 1970.
White Dynamite and the Curly Kid, Bill Martin Jr. H. Holt & Co., 1986.
Whoppers: Tall Tales and Other Lies, Alvin Schwartz. Harper & Row, 1975.
The Wild Washerwomen, John Yeoman. Crown, 1986.
The Wreck of the Zephyr, Chris Van Allsburg. Houghton Mifflin, 1983.
Zoo Doings: Animal Poems, Jack Prelutsky. Greenwillow Books, 1983.